The *Soft* REPLY

The Soft REPLY

BARLOW L. PACKER

BOOKCRAFT
Salt Lake City, Utah

Library of Congress Catalog Card Number: 97-71732
ISBN 1-57008-316-9

First Printing, 1997

Printed in the United States of America

Contents

We have no time for contention. We only have time to be about our Father's business. Contend with no man. Conduct yourselves . . . with calmness and conviction and I promise you success. . . . Ours is to conscientiously avoid being abrasive in our presentations and declarations.

—*Marvin J. Ashton*
(Ensign, *May 1978, pp. 7–8.*)

Prepare, Plant, and Perfect

Have you ever answered someone in an unkind manner? Have you ever replied sarcastically to someone who has spoken sarcastically to you? Have you ever cursed someone under your breath while honking your horn or slamming a door in anger?

In varying degrees of anger we have all given utterance to words we have regretted—either immediately or later—and wished we could retrieve.

Is it possible to become the kind of person who never uses harsh speech or even feels the need to speak unkindly? I believe so. Is there a need in our marriages, in our families, and in other relationships to avoid toxic language? Always.

This is a book about how we reply, answer, respond, rebut, or rejoin in our relationships with others. It is a book about remembering that "a soft answer turneth away wrath" (Proverbs 15:1). It is a book about helping to create, maintain, and live within a circle of Christlike conversation.

As Latter-day Saints we ought to reflect the highest standards of Christlike conversation when we speak to others, doing so in ways that exemplify patience, love, understanding, comfort, and peace. Knowing how important it is that we help each other work out our exaltation, the Lord has taught us much about the importance of how we speak to each other. This is evidenced by the multitude of references to our speech, our mouths, and our tongues that we find in our hymns, in the scriptures, and in counsel from the Brethren.

The soft reply is important because kind words can create much happiness. On the other hand, harsh words can create much unhappiness. Within one's marriage, the family, the workplace, church associations, or the neighborhood, the spoken word has the power to lift up or tear down, to heal or hurt. Feeling pain caused by words is as normal as feeling pain if you were hit with a brick. Because harsh words can be the root of other violence, if we want to maintain, enjoy, or restore peace in our lives we must create and maintain a language environment free from any form of verbal violence.

I remember laughing every time Archie Bunker called Edith a "dingbat." Now, I flinch at such expressions. As benign as that term may seem, it is anything but funny. Even a pet name, meant to communicate affection, can be toxic in a relationship if it is not respectful in content as well as in intention—and Archie Bunker's appellation for his long-suffering wife fails both tests. Hurtful words compromise important relationships, whereas soft replies have the potential of creating much joy.

The soft answer, or the soft reply, implies that we are responding to something someone else has initiated. This book is about learning to respond in ways that never injure. It is about verbally acting rather than reacting. It is about taking the initiative in creating a verbally nurturing environment. It is about lifting and strengthening others with our words. It is about applying the Golden Rule to our daily conversations.

A soft reply also implies the need to be constantly "in a preparation" (Alma 32:6) so that our temperament, character, emotions, and mood allow a Christlike response in any conversation.

The story is told about three people stranded overnight in a small boat during a rain storm. One experienced no ill effects whatsoever, the second caught a cold, and the third contracted a fatal case of pneumonia. All three experienced the same weather but all responded differently, depending on the individual's degree of health and resistance.

It's an individual matter too with conversation. We can take proven steps to strengthen and prepare our own conversational immune system; as a result, the quality of our replies will not depend on the quality of the emotional "weather." We can become someone who responds in a way that will edify, strengthen, and turn away wrath, whatever the circumstances. The soft reply is just as much a matter of preparing who we are as what we do.

Becoming an exemplar of the soft reply may require change—for some, a "mighty change" (see Alma 5:14); for others, perhaps a slight mid-course adjustment. But whether the change is large or small, our achieving mastery of the soft reply will meet head-on conversational reflexes we may have to overcome. We have to retrain certain reactions before it is "possible that [we] can lay hold upon every good thing" (Moroni 7:20).

Perfecting the soft reply may be likened to the metaphor Alma used about planting a seed:

> Now, we will compare the word [for our purposes, a soft reply] unto a seed. Now, if ye give place, that a seed may be planted in your heart, behold, if it be a true seed, or a good seed, if ye do not cast it out . . . it will begin to swell within . . . and . . . ye will begin to say . . . It must needs be that this is a good seed, or that the word is good, for it beginneth to enlarge my soul; yea, it beginneth to enlighten my understanding, yea, it beginneth to be delicious to me. (Alma 32:28.)

Look at the soft reply as one kind of seed in your life. Make it one you will plant and begin to nourish. Alma promised that "every seed bringeth forth unto its own likeness" (Alma 32:31). This is how a soft answer can actually bring forth its own likeness in others and turn away wrath, anger, enmity, and hostility. This is how a soft reply will create love, harmony, peace, kindness, and understanding.

Some of our replies will, in Alma's words, need to be "cast" out. We must often root up the undesirable that has sprouted or even grown and spread. We must then plant the good in its place.

In presenting this material I do not want to scold, accuse, or make anyone feel guilty. I am far from being a master of the soft reply, although I'm trying hard to make it part of my daily walk. I want to encourage, invite, and set a happy example. I have felt a spirit of love and kindness as I've worked on this book. I'd like you to feel it too.

I believe that as we root up that which should be cast out, and prepare and plant the seeds of the soft reply, "by [our] faith . . . great diligence, and with patience," we will find ourselves "looking forward to the fruit thereof." We will come to know that the soft reply is one seed that will take root and, if nourished, will be perfected as a "tree springing up unto everlasting life." (Alma 32:41.)

*I speak to fathers and mothers everywhere with a plea to
put harshness behind us, to bridle our anger, to lower
our voices, and to deal with mercy and love and respect
one toward another in our homes. . . . Let us be more
compassionate, gentler, filled with forbearance and
patience and a greater measure of respect one for another.*

—Gordon B. Hinckley
(Ensign, *May 1990, p. 70.)*

Moving to Knowledge: Level 2

Life blesses us with experiences that bring an awareness of
what matters most. At such times we understand principles of life
that are indelibly written on our souls. We're not always able to
apply these lessons immediately, but we never forget them. I thank
God for such moments, because their memory keeps us ever more
aware of the course we must follow even when the routines and
frustrations of daily life confuse us. For me, one such benchmark
experience occurred on 17 July 1964.

It was my wedding day. I arrived at Margaret's house early so we
could drive to the temple together on this day that was so special
for both of us.

Before we left her house, however, Margaret's parents wanted to
take a picture of the two of us standing on the front porch. With
his camera, Margaret's father positioned himself at just the right
spot on the lawn in front of the porch. He put his glasses down on

the grass so he could focus his camera. We smiled. "One, two, three," he counted; then he snapped the picture.

I offered to take a picture of Margaret and her parents. Her father came to the porch. I moved down to the lawn, camera in hand. I took up my position exactly where he had been standing and looked through the camera to make a minute adjustment to the focus. I stepped back just a step. *Crunch!* I felt and heard the glass beneath me. I had just smashed my future father-in-law's glasses to bits. Great way to begin a relationship!

I was humiliated, anxious, and terribly apologetic. Margaret's father smiled and put a hand on my arm. "Don't worry about it," he said softly. "I'll get by." There was no anger, no rebuke, no reprisal. Just acceptance and calm.

A couple of hours later we were in the temple. Margaret's father must have had to squint to see how beautiful his daughter looked as we sat next to each other surrounded by friends and family. A wonderful spirit filled the room with peace and love. I wondered what the feeling in the room might have been if my father-in-law had snapped at me about his broken glasses and rubbed in the inconvenience I had caused him during this important family day. I will always be grateful to him for his soft replies then and since.

As Elder Gordon B. Hinckley counseled us before performing the wedding ceremony, his words were inspiring, simple, and very fundamental. There were just four things he asked us to remember:

1. *Always pray together as a couple both morning and night.*

I thought, "We can do that." Prayer was very important to both of us. We always prayed individually both night and morning. Praying together would be natural, almost instinctive. We would simply merge our common habits.

2. *Always show mutual respect.*

"Okay," I thought. "That means always showing courtesy and sensitivity for Margaret's thoughts and values. How could I do anything else?" Looking back, I realize that I was perhaps overoptimistic about both my abilities and my performance.

3. *Always be financially honest with the Lord.*

Paying tithing and other offerings was something we not only did individually already but strongly felt constituted a blessing to us. I felt confident about our ability to keep this counsel, as well; truth to tell, it has not been a difficult commandment to follow, even at times when money was tight.

4. *Always remember the soft reply.*

Here Elder Hinckley led me into new territory—although I'm sure Margaret was already very familiar with the terrain. In a few precious moments he taught us this principle about how we should speak to each other as husband and wife. A few years later Margaret and I were grateful when he returned to the subject during one of his conference addresses:

> We seldom get into trouble when we speak softly. It is only when we raise our voices that the sparks fly and tiny molehills become great mountains of contention. To me there has always been something significant in the description of the prophet Elijah's contest with the priests of Baal. The scripture records that "a great and strong wind rent the mountains, and brake in pieces the rocks . . . but the Lord was not in the wind: and after the wind an earthquake; but the Lord was not in the earthquake: and after the earthquake a fire; but the Lord was not in the fire: and after the fire a still small voice." (I Kings 19:11–12.)
>
> The voice of heaven is a still small voice; likewise, the voice of domestic peace is a quiet voice.[1]

As I listened on our wedding day to Elder Hinckley's counsel about the soft reply, I thought: "No problem. How could I ever bark or snap at Margaret, this wonderful person whom I love with all my heart, whose hand I am holding in this beautiful room?"

Although my parents, like Margaret's, had emphasized the importance of clean and kindly speech in our home and unsheathed the equivalent of a terrible swift sword when it came to name-calling, when President Hinckley gave his counsel it was the first time I could remember being specifically taught to choose a soft voice when making a contribution to a family dialogue. It was the beginning of what will be a lifelong effort to more deeply learn about and follow President Hinckley's counsel.

Our knowledge progresses through three levels: (1) We don't know what it is we don't know. (2) We know what it is we don't know. And (3) we know what it is we know.

As I look back on the counsel we received on our wedding day, I realize that I was young and well-intentioned but also was very much nestled into Level I—I didn't know what it was I didn't know, especially about how my use of the soft reply would affect my marriage, my children, my friendships, and my career. It wasn't for several years, until after Margaret's father had passed away, that I fully realized how well he had modeled the soft reply that morning. He had treated me in the very manner that an Apostle of the Lord counseled me to treat Margaret.

Ever since then, raising our children and refining our marriage has intensified my perception of what it means for me to give and receive a soft reply. I have been made aware of how much and how often the Lord teaches us about this principle. Have I always practiced the soft reply? Hardly! But because of my awareness of and my determination to follow President Hinckley's counsel, my marriage, family, business, and social relationships have been greatly blessed, to the degree that I have been able to live by what I call the miracle of the soft reply. Like most matters in life, however, knowing and doing are two different things. But at least I have moved from Level 1 to Level 2. I at least know what it is I don't know about the soft reply.

NOTES

1. Gordon B. Hinckley, "Except the Lord Build the House . . ." *Ensign*, June 1971, p. 72.

CHAPTER 2

A man who cannot control his temper is not very likely to control his passions, and no matter what his pretensions in religion, he moves in daily life very close to the animal plane. . . . It is the attitude of the person during the daily contacts by which we show whether we are appealing to the carnal or to the spiritual within us and within those with whom we associate.

—*David O. McKay*
(Improvement Era, *December 1963, p. 1096.)*

An Experience with Rolex Arrogance

As Margaret and I began our marriage we immediately dived into the challenges of graduate school, developing a career, establishing a net worth, starting a family, and growing in the gospel. Time passed; and in my efforts to become successful in my career I was exposed to many theories on how one becomes "successful"—this from a variety of tapes, books, and professional seminars. (A few of these authors, I now realize, were "successful" only because thousands of people like me bought their books and tapes.) Even though there are many definitions of "success," I read and listened and tried to apply the principles I thought were worthwhile.

Little by little, Margaret and I were blessed in many ways. In a few years we were able to buy a comfortable home in a pleasant suburban neighborhood. It was a two-story house on a sloping lot, with a deck overlooking the city and a view of the mountains.

I can remember one beautiful spring Saturday morning when I stood on the deck enjoying the view and feeling very successful. I was, in a sense, surveying my kingdom. My practice was growing. I had many trusting patients. I was honestly trying to serve them well, and I tried always to be kind. I was also actively involved in my Church callings. Margaret was a wonderful wife and my best friend. I was proud of my five children. They practiced the piano, kept their rooms clean, did their homework, and yes, most of the time even helped with the dishes.

That particular morning, however, my fourteen-year-old son had just finished mowing the lawn. Being somewhat inexperienced with a power mower, he had nicked a sprinkler head or two with the rotary mower blade. As I turned on the sprinkler system to water, two or three fountains of water shot into the air like mini-geysers.

I was irritated with my son and exasperated by this hitch in my plans. I looked at my Rolex, mentally calculating how much time it was going to take to repair the sprinklers. I became more upset.

I began to lecture my son, telling him just how upset I was and then moving on to how inconsiderate he was. "Why can't you be more careful?" I demanded rhetorically. I also added a few toxic comments about how little he knew about operating power mowers. With each comment my voice grew louder and harsher; and as I turned toward the car to drive to the hardware store I hissed through clenched teeth something about "stupid" and "jerk."

A few minutes later, on my way to the store, I noticed that my rage had subsided. In the pit of my stomach was a sinking feeling. I didn't feel "successful." I felt awful. And it wasn't the first time I'd had this feeling.

In his book *The Kingship of Self-Control*, William George Jordan says: "The second most deadly instrument of destruction is the gun—the first is the human tongue. . . . The havoc of the gun is visible at once, the full evil of the tongue lives through all the years."[1]

It was not difficult to realize that no matter what watch I was wearing, what house I lived in, or what car I drove, I could not be successful in the ways I most wanted to if I could not master the words that came from my mouth. The personality I had unleashed on my son was only a manifestation of pride and Rolex-like arrogance.

I was troubled not only by that but also by the Savior's warning: "Every idle word that men shall speak, they shall give account thereof in the day of judgment" (Matthew 12:36).

I groaned within myself and renewed my commitment to follow President Hinckley's call to perfect the soft reply. No matter how often I slipped backwards, I wanted to develop a more Christlike, finished character. I wanted to experience the "mighty change" inherent in President Hinckley's "soft answer" counsel and separate myself from the poisonous verbal traditions of the world. With the desire to partake more of Christ's divine nature, I began the climb again.

As soon as I returned home, even before repairing the sprinkler heads, I took my son aside and apologized for the way I had treated him. It is not easy to apologize to one of your children, but doing so taught me three things. First, our children are very forgiving. Second, they really can understand that adults make mistakes. And third, it made it easier to apologize in the future—and this lesson was perhaps the most useful of them all. Over the years my willingness to apologize when necessary has strengthened our relationship. Not only has my children's forgiveness brought me peace and increased the love in our family but also I have felt good about modeling an excellent way to show mutual respect. The common courtesy of extending a deserved apology is a wonderful form of the soft reply that should not have any age restrictions.

So I added my Saturday Sprinkler Revelation to my Wedding Day Revelation. Days like this taught me to know what it was I didn't know. I had always said that sprinkler heads were not as important as relationships, but this knowledge had become my own because I had acted on it. The irritating geysers from my sprinkling system had become a peaceful and joy-giving taste of that living water, "springing up into everlasting life" (John 4:14).

NOTES

1. As quoted by Thorpe B. Isaacson in *Improvement Era*, June 1964, p. 501.

CHAPTER 3

*So in the give-and-take in the kingdom, we
jostle and are jostled. . . . Let us all take extra
care to avoid both giving and taking offense.
Let us be loving, kind, and forgiving . . . ,
grounded, rooted, established, and settled.*

—Neal A. Maxwell
(Ensign, *May 1982, p. 39.*)

Escaping the "Blender" World

And then there was the Sunday Blender Revelation. It was early in the morning when I walked down the hall toward the kitchen, but as I came around the corner I saw that someone was up before me. Our three-year-old son was sitting on the floor in front of the sink. Pots and pans were scattered everywhere, and on the floor in front of him was the blender. The base with all the control buttons was wedged between his tiny legs, the plastic container in place. He was holding the plug in his little hand, scanning the perimeter for some place to plug it in.

Inside the blender chamber, filling it to the brim, was the entire population of his little wooden Fisher-Price village people. (You know the little guys I'm talking about because there is one lost in every couch in America.) Had he had a couple more seconds to locate a plug and push the "Puree" button, an entire community would have been reduced to sawdust.

I squatted down by my boy and said: "Hey, fella. Let's try this instead." I gave him a large stainless steel mixing bowl into which the Fisher-Price folks clattered satisfyingly and I put the blender's deadly blades out of the reach of those chubby little fingers. Through the whole experience the Fisher-Price folk smiled on.

Sometimes the world seems just like that—the whole population tumbled together in a huge blender, with fate or destiny ready to throw the switch. I find heroic the many people who manage to be kind and generous, in spite of it all, most of the time. While making their way through life's daily grind they keep a Fisher-Price smile, even when it seems as if fate's hand is poised on the blender switch. These folks have managed to develop and maintain a serenity of thought and speech despite the enmity around them. They have learned to act rather than react or let themselves be acted upon.

I've come to believe that there must be a way of living in this sometimes blender-like world and of handling the daily grind without turning into sawdust. There must be a way to keep that smile in spite of it all. In the words of Ella Wheeler Wilcox:

> It is easy enough to be pleasant
> When life flows by like a song.
> But the man worth while is one who will smile
> When everything goes dead wrong.

Daily life can be a frustrating challenge to everyone at times. Life can be a grind, stressful, and taxing to our patience. During these tense moments, kindness, tolerance, and good humor tend to wane; and our "softer side" disappears. When we let the grind get to us we are often less than kind to loved ones and friends. When we view ourselves as powerless, helpless to stop what's happening to us, we naturally try to assert ourselves in an attempt to regain control. Sometimes we growl at others in making the attempt.

The little Fisher-Price people were truly helpless, but we are not wooden toys. We must never let ourselves believe that we cannot control our own attitude. We must not lay on a circumstance of the moment or the day the responsibility for how we feel or talk. I love the instruction the Lord gives us about seeing ourselves as agents with the ability to act, not as helpless victims of circumstances or of other people's actions.

> And now, my sons, I speak unto you these things for your profit and learning; for there is a God, and he hath created all things, both the heavens and the earth, and all things that in them are, both things to act and things to be acted upon.
>
> And to bring about his eternal purposes in the end of man . . . it must needs be that there was an opposition; even the forbidden fruit in opposition to the tree of life; the one being sweet and the other bitter.
>
> Wherefore, the Lord God gave unto man that he should act for himself. Wherefore, man could not act for himself save it should be that he was enticed by the one or the other. (2 Nephi 2:14–16.)

It is all too common today for people who have been offended to respond in kind, returning offense for offense because they felt "acted upon." A politician tells a tasteless joke and an entire ethnic group is offended and protests. Someone cut off in traffic expresses displeasure by using profanity and rude gestures. A gardener finds a neighbor's pet roaming his flower bed, and heated words accelerate rapidly to insults and even threats.

We live in an intemperate time, one that is fraught with anger and contention. Nation is pitted against nation, corporation against corporation, neighbor against neighbor, parents against children, spouse against spouse. All these relationships, which should be nurturing, are too often hostile. Because they see themselves as powerless many feel justified in counterattacking viciously with any weapon that comes to hand. Such an immoderate and unethical reaction is a confession that we truly do feel helpless. We feel justified in striking back, with no holds barred, because we don't believe that anything we can do will really hurt our target.

But even a moment's thought shows how dangerous such an attitude is. The fact is that we have great power to injure others, and the targets of our wrath often suffer untold damage. When as individuals we let ourselves be acted upon we choose to let those feelings trigger reactions and overreactions we will later regret.

As human beings, as sons and daughters of God, we have within us the power and God-given ability to choose either the Spirit that leads us to do good or the spirit that leads us to do evil. For example, say you have had a frustrating day filled with unpleasant situations, and you have been choking back the anger. Coming home you realize that one of the children (or something else) could precipitate a flash point. You might end up unloading on a member of your family. Aware of your own limitations, you can take a simple preventive measure I have tried to use over the years. When you come in the door, announce calmly: "I've had a bad day. I think I'm at the exploding point and just need a few minutes to unwind. I'm going into the den, and when I come out I'll be Daddy, not a grouch." This approach means that you are choosing to act rather than just letting something happen. It is one way of taking control.

I believe that when we choose to act rather than let ourselves be acted upon our consciences will always guide us to behave in a more Christlike manner. Wouldn't you always choose to act and speak kindly, no matter what the circumstance, if you could really choose? Blender world or not, it is within our power to make a soft reply.

CHAPTER 4

Have the same courtesy in your homes that you
have when you are out in society. Thank your
wives; thank your children; and say, "If you
please," "Excuse me." These little things mean
so much and make life so much sweeter.

—David O. McKay
(Improvement Era, *December 1968, p. 109.)*

The Butterfly Effect

I feel that refining the soft reply, whether to those we love or those we don't even know, will always be one measure of our character growth and spiritual development. Unfortunately, by this measure society's character and spiritual development are in pretty bad shape. Verbal abuse, sarcasm, and yelling have become epidemic. We read about it in newspapers, in magazines. We see it on TV. And it is sad that we all too often see it at home and at work.

One important key to controlling how we speak to others is recognizing that every word we emit has its beginning first in thought; hence to change what we say will ultimately require that we change how we think. The waterfall of words that may wash away a relationship was a tiny spring of thought a moment before. Unfortunately, most people can think much faster than they can talk, which provides an inexhaustible bank account of words the mouth can never overdraw. If the eyes are the windows to the soul, it might be said that the mouth is its radio, often broadcasting uncensored and uncontrolled runaway thoughts.

Listening to information on talk radio has become a popular pastime for many in America. Everything from sports to politics is discussed freely as people call in and enjoy the rush that comes from being able to sound off over the air. The broadcast is electronically delayed five or six seconds to give the host a modicum of control, since Federal Communications Commission restrictions forbid some inappropriate forms of expression. The host has a button that allows him to immediately cut off a caller so that between speaking and broadcasting there is the space of a few seconds.

How nice it would be if we were all equipped with a similar electronic delay mechanism between the brain and the mouth to prevent the damaging transmissions. But we aren't. The only button we have is the principle of practice. All we can really do is practice, practice, practice. As James Allen wrote: "Just as an artisan becomes, by practice, accomplished in his craft, so a man can become, by practice, accomplished in goodness; it is entirely a matter of forming new habits of thought." We might apply his words to the soft reply: "There is no more secret about its acquirement than about any other acquisition, for it is governed by the underlying principle of all development, namely, practice. To be able to do a thing, you must begin to do it, and keep on doing it until the thing is mastered."[1] Therefore we must begin today and practice daily, refining the control of thought and emotion that will perfect the soft reply.

Because of the effect even the smallest comment can have, we must never forget how important it is to learn to control what we say. The new science of CHAOS has coined an expression called the butterfly effect. It suggests that a butterfly stirring the air today in Peking can transform a storm system next month in New York. This is another way of saying that everything is connected. It is a scientific equivalent of the Lord's expression, "Out of small things proceedeth that which is great" (D&C 64:33). Whether it is one beat of a butterfly's wings or a single word, harshly spoken, the effect of our words can be dramatic and extremely damaging if they are not controlled.

The Lord cautions us through King Benjamin: "But this much I can tell you, that if ye do not watch yourselves, and your thoughts, and your words . . . even unto the end of your lives, ye must perish. And now, O man, remember, and perish not." (Mosiah 4:30.)

Controlling how we speak to others and mastery of the soft reply is something each person can begin to perfect now, today—in one's very next conversation. Gradually the growth necessary to achieve a more Christlike level in our thoughts and the words they generate will be accomplished through a series of single successes. Fortunately, with the soft reply, if one time we stumble we can pick ourselves up and put ourselves "in a preparation" to succeed the next time. Little by little, by acting in ways that are consistent with our Christlike ideals and goals, we will become the person we hope to become. This kind of transformation doesn't involve changing the masses, but just oneself. As we practice we will gradually be able to master our tongues and the harsh things we are tempted to say. We will have developed greater restraint and awareness because we have hit the practice button so many times before.

Ultimately we will develop the ability to not even feel or think harsh things, thus guaranteeing they will never be said. It is then that we will no longer need delay mechanisms or buttons, because our words will have become evidence of Christlike thoughts. Restraint is not necessary when there is nothing inappropriate to hold back.

NOTES

1. James Allen, *As a Man Thinketh, Volume 2* James H. Fedor, ed. (Bountiful, Utah: Mind Art, 1988), pp. 73, 93.

CHAPTER 5

Practice speaking in a soft, calm voice. The peaceful life can best be attained not by those who speak with a voice of "great tumultuous noise" but by those who follow the Savior's example and speak with "a still voice of perfect mildness."

—Marvin J. Ashton
(Ensign, May 1978, p. 9.)

Practice Makes Perfect

Many Latter-day Saints wear CTR rings that date from Primary days, sometimes in the language of their mission field. The letters CTR, embossed on a shield-shaped field, remind the wearer that "when a choice is placed before [us]" we are to "choose the right."[1]

Each day offers many moments when we may choose between an irritable answer and a soft reply. Sometimes we have only an instant to respond, but here's a technique to help us choose better. We can anticipate difficult situations and rehearse a better answer than an irritable reflex might spontaneously produce.

In major league baseball each pitcher's technique is analyzed— by sight, in video playback, and even with computerized images. What pitch is most often his first pitch? What pitches are his most common with two strikes or three balls on the batter? The batter has only an instant after the ball leaves the pitcher's hand to anticipate where and how it will be coming. His odds of getting a hit increase dramatically if he can outguess the pitcher. The same principle is useful when a circumstance is "thrown" at us and we must decide quickly how we will respond.

Following are some typical stressful situations that I have adapted slightly from a test list that was seeking participants' responses.[2] The choices are obviously simple—either relaxed and soft or irritable and stressful. There's no question about which answer is the best one in each case, but visualize yourself turning away from the irritable response and rehearsing the soft reply in each circumstance. Notice particularly how it makes you feel inside to "choose the right"—or soft—reply.

1. A teenage boy pulls up beside me at a stop light, his car stereo blasting acid rock.
   a. I chuckle inside as I reflect on why teenagers can't hear.
   b. I want to yell at him to turn it down.
2. My barber gives me a haircut that is much shorter than I wanted.
   a. I curtly tell him he did a lousy job.
   b. I think: "Hair grows out. I must be a little clearer with my instructions next time."
3. I am in a line at the express checkout at the supermarket. The sign reads Ten Items Only, and I see someone ahead of me with fifteen.
   a. I say something to that person or complain to the clerk when it's my turn.
   b. I pick up the latest issue of *Life Magazine* from the magazine rack to pass the time.
4. I am stuck in the middle of freeway gridlock.
   a. I start to mumble and complain under my breath at all the other "lousy" drivers.
   b. I put in a cassette tape, relax, and try to enjoy the moment.
5. An elevator I am waiting for takes an extra long time arriving at my floor.

    a. I keep impatiently punching and repunching the down button, even though it is still lit.

    b. I take a few minutes to review my schedule for the day or catch a couple of paragraphs from the book in my briefcase.

6. Someone is speaking very slowly during a conversation on a topic I know a lot about.

    a. I keep butting in and finishing their sentences for them.

    b. I politely listen.

7. The person with a seat on the same row as mine wants to get out to the aisle for the umpteenth time during a ball game.

    a. I make some sarcastic comment after he has passed and is not quite out of hearing range.

    b. I smile, stand so he can pass, and take the opportunity to stretch my legs.

8. I overhear the person just in front of me in line at the bank inform the teller that she would like to buy $500 worth of traveler checks in $50 denominations.

    a. I groan loudly enough to be heard.

    b. I politely ask if I might go first, or I decide to take my chances in another line.

9. I am out with another couple who occupy the entire evening going on and on about their new granddaughter.

    a. I constantly keep trying to change the subject.

    b. I politely listen and try to become interested.

10. A very overweight person in my dinner group orders a banana split for dessert.

    a. I later make a sarcastic comment to someone else in the group.

    b. I empathize with the challenges of a possible metabolic defect or psychological problem.

Our responses at moments like these reveal either our degree of cynicism, anger, and aggression or our degree of compassion, patience, and understanding. Rehearsing possible responses in advance prepares us to choose the soft reply. None of these incidents is particularly important, but they help us rehearse for those occasions when a relationship depends on a gentle response.

We are all human, so we are all at risk when it comes to choosing how we will reply. But one thing is certain: Whatever the situation, your choice will never be a wrong choice if you always choose the softest of all choices placed before you. In other words, CTSR—choose the soft reply.

NOTES

1. "Choose the Right," *Hymns,* no. 239.

2. See Redford Williams, M.D., and Virginia Williams, Ph.D., *Anger Kills* (New York: Harper Perennial, 1993), pp. 5–11.

CHAPTER 6

No one needs to be grouchy. No one needs to be unpleasant. Everyone can control his emotions if he wants to, just as he can control his appetites.

—*Mark E. Petersen*
(Improvement Era, *December 1961, p. 941.*)

Engaging the Brain Before We Speak

There is a neurological phenomenon known as the thalamic reaction.[1] Thalamic reactions are responses we make to certain stimuli that are registered by the thalamus instead of the cortex area of the brain. Thalamic reactions, it could be said, are things we do or say without thinking first, things that are reflexive, reactive, habitual, or done at a subconscious level. If you are out walking and accidentally trip, without your thinking your muscles are put into action instantaneously to keep you from falling.

The thalamus is designed for use in times of danger, for "fight or flight." As to the soft reply, unfortunately we often see verbal "danger" where it doesn't exist, and so we speak in a reactive manner, "spouting off" without thinking. Thalamic reaction is most likely to happen when we are under pressure, running late, or feel used, as well as when we see someone in danger.

On the other hand, the part of the brain that governs conscious response, the cortex, is where we do our logical thinking and planning. As we receive incoming stimuli, meaning, or information, especially of a verbal nature, we frequently fail to let the cortex consider everything and we then speak without thinking. Failure to take time to think before we say something is one of the most common causes of a communication breakdown. This can result in harsh words, arguments, fights, domestic quarrels, and verbal abuse.

If we will allow it to do so, the cortex can sort sensory impressions and correlate them with memories stored there. The cortex's critical function is to weigh various courses of action against each other and allow us to make a thoughtful decision about how to respond.

Sometimes the thalamus—and I'm not sure why—in effect short-circuits the cortex or cuts it out of the loop. I remember once standing in line at an airport gate counter to receive a boarding pass for a better seat on the airplane. I saw someone crowd in the line ahead of me. Without thinking, I loudly shouted something. Afterwards I wished I had kept my mouth shut, but it was as if I couldn't help myself. In other words, I didn't stop and think about it first.

Our awareness of this possibility, something that I'm sure has happened to all of us, will help us aspire to and perfect a soft reply. If we can practice and develop the ability to pause for a moment, then count to ten—or even to one or two—we will likely respond differently. The whole process requires only an instant as we let the cortex take over and govern our response.

A word of caution is necessary, however. Even though soft speech can *never* be a thalamic reaction, not all cortical responses are acceptable. Hence we must be careful not to admire derogatory examples of cortical cleverness and make a place for them in our speech. We must realize that often the most biting response can also be thought out. This kind of reply is prompted by malice aforethought, like a mean letter to the editor. It is also the kind of hurtful put-down or zinger we are exposed to on so many inane television programs. The fact that a response is cortical doesn't necessarily mean it is uplifting and soft.

If we can allow our cortex to get "up to speed," however, we have a greater chance more often of responding softly than if we succumb to thalamic reactions. The effect of those reactions upon marriages, families, and the workplace can be devastating. Many people are looking for a new spouse or a new job because of thalamic override that manifests itself in the form of anger and sarcasm.

The soft answer will triumph, but to ensure this we must pause, engage the mind, and speak thoughtfully soft rather than react without thinking. Sometimes it is just a simple matter of being nice. Elder Hartman Rector, Jr., in his final general conference address, said it so well: "Yes, we must be nice. If we're not nice, I don't think we're going to make it."[2]

NOTES

1. See Omer K. Reed, *Reed's International Letter, Quarterly,* January 1993, pp. 2–3.

2. Hartman Rector, Jr., "Endure to the End in Charity," *Ensign,* November 1994, p. 26.

I invite all members of the Church to live with ever more attention to the life and example of the Lord Jesus Christ, especially the love and hope and compassion he displayed. I pray that we will treat each other with more kindness, more patience, more courtesy and forgiveness.

—*Howard W. Hunter*
(Ensign, *November 1994, p. 8.)*

Overcoming "Knee-Jerk" Replies

If we fail to use a soft reply when we should use it, it is often because of anger, which, as Benjamin Franklin said, is "never without a reason, but seldom with a good one."[1] One of the reasons why we lose control, make the wrong choice, and say the wrong thing is that we often just let things happen. We let the hostility of the natural man preside over the moment because we fail to anticipate or prepare, in advance, strategies or contingency plans.

In their book *Anger Kills*, as I've already explained, Redford and Virginia Williams talk about rehearsing responses to stressful situations as a simple strategy for defusing hostility. They also suggest other useful strategies for keeping emotional control instead of turning loose the thalamic reaction of rage.[2]

1. Reason with yourself. Frequently one of the reasons why we become angry is that our momentary perception of the problem makes it larger than it really is. How many times have we heard the

expression, "Don't sweat the small stuff"? The fact is that most matters we become upset over are small stuff. Train yourself to recognize the emotion of irritation and anger. When you sense irritation as an emotional response to a situation, ask yourself: "How much does this really matter?" You can often talk yourself out of harsh feelings—and harsh responses—as a result.

You might try this the next time one of the children has just tracked mud in on your freshly mopped kitchen floor. Exploding might make you feel better for the moment, but if you do it you'll feel bad later on, and the floor will still be muddy. When you ask yourself "How much does this really matter?" you'll be able to see quickly that your relationship with your child matters more but that it is also important for your child to learn two things: (1) the habit of wiping his shoes, and (2) the habit of cleaning up after himself. Without being angry or threatening, you can help your child go through the motions of both lessons, motions that he will have to repeat many times before either of them becomes a habit.

2. Find a distraction. My father used to say "Bite your tongue" when he could tell I was tempted to say a rash or hasty thing. It's true that pain can be a distraction, but it's a lot less wearing to choose something undamaging. If a noisy person behind you in the theater is driving you to the brink of making a sarcastic comment, why not go out for popcorn or change seats if you don't feel you can politely ask the person to stop talking? The old proverb of counting to ten is another effective distraction. Thomas Jefferson, in his Ten Canons of Conduct, said: "When angry, count ten before you speak; if very angry, an hundred."[3] Almost anything will work as a distraction: open a magazine, shuffle some papers, leave the room, turn on the car radio, walk to the sink and get a glass of water, or pet the dog.

3. Remember it is sometimes okay to intervene on your own behalf. Channeling frustration by being appropriately assertive allows you to handle many situations, remain courteous, but still accomplish your task. If you are waiting to use the photocopier for

two items and the person ahead of you has six books bristling with bookmarks, why not politely say: "I've just got two pages. Would you mind if I went first?" Or if you have been waiting for fifteen minutes to sign up for your discount shopping card and the clerk starts to help the person to your left or right who just walked up, you might calmly say to her, "I know things are really crowded, but I believe I was next."

Once I needed a radio knob for our VW bug and went to the dealership parts department to buy one. I was about sixth in a line at the parts counter, where one clerk was trying to wait on us and handle the phone at the same time.

I stood there for about ten minutes as the same scenario was repeated over and over. The phone would ring. The clerk would pick it up and answer, "Parts Department." He would listen for a minute and then say, "Just a minute, I'll check." He would then disappear down an aisle between the shelves of parts, reappear a minute or so later, pick up the phone, and say, "Yes, we have that part in stock." Sometimes he would even look up the price. Then he would hang up the phone, ask the person in front of him what part he needed (sometimes for the second or third time), and then be interrupted again by the ringing of the phone.

People in the line became testy, grumbling a little under their breath. I found myself shifting from foot to foot and checking my watch. The clerk was doing his best, but he couldn't do two jobs at once and he had for some reason decided that the ringing phone had top priority.

I could see I was in for a long wait to get my one little knob. Then I noticed a public pay phone about twenty feet away. I left my place in line, went over to the pay phone, looked up the number of the Parts Department, and dialed. Sure enough, the phone on the counter rang. The young man picked it up.

"Parts Department."

"Do you have a radio on-off knob for a '69 VW bug?"

"Just a minute, I'll check."

"If you do, will you bring it to the counter? I'll be right there, and you won't have to hunt for it again."

I watched him put down the phone. The line of waiting people grumbled as he disappeared. In a minute or two he reappeared with the knob in his hand. I instantly hung up and walked to the counter. Before he could pick up the phone to tell me he had the knob, I said: "I'm the guy who just called about that knob."

I'll never forget the look on his face as he put it all together. Then I said sympathetically, "It's tough handling all this alone, isn't it?"

"Wow!" was his response.

He was still holding the phone, which by then was emitting a dial tone. I asked in the same sympathetic voice: "What would happen if you left that thing off the hook for a few minutes?"

Almost in unison, the other people in line exclaimed, "Yes!"

It suddenly dawned on the clerk that a caller, getting a busy signal, would simply call back in a few minutes. Triumphantly, he raised the phone receiver above his head and then set it down firmly on the counter. You could feel the mood of frustration in the line dissolve, to be replaced by delight and patience. My intervention had solved my own problem and made things better for everyone, including the beleaguered clerk.

4. Withdraw or lower your expectations. Redford and Virginia Williams call this technique trusting others. At work I often think that a task, to be done right, has to be done my way. Although my employees seldom say anything, I know they feel put down as I butt in to supervise, micromanage, and interfere. I've found that it's possible to decide to deliberately not have expectations about how someone will do a job I delegate to him or her, as long as I've communicated expectations about how it will look when it's done. It's amazing. I stop feeling the urge to make suggestions or hover around to get the person started. I stop being amazed that they can't read my mind. I stop being frustrated when the job is broken into different steps than I would have used. It's just okay for them to do it the way that seems best. Focusing on the result and not the process makes both my employee and me feel better.

5. Forgive. Again, I've been amazed by the discovery that it's possible to practice saying, "It's all right" when I feel disappointed about a product, a process, or an interaction. Naturally there are times when something is really important to me and a failure is *not* all right. We all need to develop other techniques for handling those situations. But being able to say to myself or someone else, "It's all right," is enormously liberating. These simple but profound words liberate me from resentment, nagging, put-downs, or sarcasm. Maybe your steak ended up well done when you wanted it medium rare. Maybe you can't start family home evening because you're waiting for one of the children to get off the phone. Maybe you bring a new acquaintance along to introduce to a couple of your best friends at lunch, and she ends up dominating the conversation.

You feel your temperature rising. But is there some deliberate plot to "get" you? Is this person consciously trying to annoy you? Hardly ever. Yes, you might have been inconvenienced or delayed. But the simple will to forgive a person who has offended you is the most Christlike thing anyone can do in such a situation and will mellow harsh feelings, change you from within, and generate soft reply after soft reply. It is what you could call the seventy times seventy strategy.

NOTES

1. *Poor Richard's Almanac*, 1754.

2. See Williams and Williams, *Anger Kills*, pp. 66, 82, 100, 127, 158.

3. John Bartlett, *Familiar Quotations*, 14th ed. (Boston: Little, Brown and Company, 1968), p. 474.

CHAPTER **8**

Affection for "Stuff" Versus People

Controlling our speech is easier if we are able to keep an eternal perspective. And one way to maintain an eternal perspective is to maintain a proper attitude toward material possessions.

One night I was sitting in my car outside the restaurant where my son worked, waiting to take him home. I watched a young man in another car start to back out of his parking space. A couple had stopped their car to wait for the vacated stall. Not watching carefully enough, the young man backed into the waiting car. It was a very slight bump. The only damage was a small crack in the plastic license plate frame. You can buy one for ten dollars at any auto parts store.

The young man was embarrassed and very apologetic. He offered immediately to replace the frame or give the older man money to get a new one, but the other driver began berating the young man, swearing and yelling at him so obnoxiously that a small crowd gathered. The man's wife slumped down in her seat, obviously humiliated and upset. I assumed that this was not the first scene of this type she had been subjected to.

Two other men, apparently sensing the possibility that this older man might actually become violent, stepped up quietly and stood behind the young man without saying anything. Still furious, the older driver returned to his car and departed, punctuating his exit with an obscene gesture. His wife had slumped so far down in the front seat that she was barely visible.

I reflected uncomfortably on the episode of the nicked sprinkler heads and realized that a cracked window, a ding in my car door, a lost basketball, a bike left out in the rain, a broken dish, muddy footprints, or a defective purchase had also been equally inconsequential catalysts for less than Christlike behavior on my part. I was ashamed of myself, ashamed of this man, and ashamed that our love of material things could provoke the use of this kind of hurtful and poisonous language.

When we erupt over "stuff" it is an indication that we have let our possessions become symbols of our personal worth. The oft-repeated cycle of destruction in the Nephites' civilization usually began with an inordinate love of "stuff." It manifested itself in being "lifted up in pride, such as the wearing of costly apparel, and all manner of fine pearls, and of the fine things of the world." From this they progressed to "build[ing] up churches unto themselves to get gain, . . . smit[ing] upon the people of Jesus." (4 Nephi 1:24, 26, 34.) It is not unrealistic to suggest that they began their march to the carnage of the final battlefields when they began yielding their hearts to the tyranny of "stuff."

It does not matter whether our possessions are numerous or few, expensive or inexpensive, stylish or out of date—none of them can give us pleasure after our mortal life is over. Why, then, do we spend our few years of mortality acting as if we believe the only way to be happy is to accumulate more and more of this world's goods?

Hugh Nibley describes this feverish materialism as manifested in America's TV programs:

> All day long, and half the night, a procession of plots, murders, bedrooms, fights, and lethal explosions passes before the bemused spectator, sharing time with cunningly calculated interruptions by lavishly contrived commercial sideshows . . . and the [motive] that runs through it all is *money.* . . . The less important an object is, . . . the more fervidly and persistently it must be brought to the public's attention, so that what the new generation gets is a world turned upside down, with the froth as the substance and foundation of reality. . . . We have a complete switch of values.[1]

Along with this, an affection for *things* can displace an affection for *people,* lessening the constraints on our toxic language and increasing the potential for violence. The antidote for love of stuff is a deliberate, chosen simplicity. Laurence Peter, author of *The Peter Principle,* and his wife began thoughtfully to search for a peaceful balance between the material and nonmaterial parts of their life. Unexpectedly, they found that this principle-centered approach paid dividends they could not have anticipated. For example, Peter replaced their cheap power mower with a high-quality hand mower and discovered a long list of frustrations that this single decision eliminated: "It never runs out of fuel. It never tests my patience getting it started. It emits no pollutants. It provides me with healthful exercise. I can stop and start it with ease. I feel in control. I feel relieved of the nervous strain, the safety hazards, and the inevitable mechanical problems and responsibilities that power equipment entails."[2]

The things that make us conten-ted rather than conten-tious come from a keen sense of enjoying the moment, a deepened appreciation of ordinary pleasures, and the company of affectionate, loving friends and family. One person called it the only way to be rich.

In the final analysis, the only things we can take with us into the next life are the knowledge we have acquired and the personal relationships we have cultivated. Moroni understood this truth when he asked, "Why do ye adorn yourselves with that which hath no life?" (Mormon 8:39.)

NOTES

1. Hugh Nibley, *Approaching Zion* (Salt Lake City: Deseret Book, 1989), pp. 535–36.

2. As quoted in Marilyn Ferguson, *The Aquarian Conspiracy* (Los Angeles: J. P. Tarcher, 1987), p. 339.

CHAPTER 9

Whenever you get red in the face, whenever you raise your voice, whenever you get "hot under the collar," or angry, . . . know that the Spirit of God is leaving you and the spirit of Satan is beginning to take over. At times we may feel justified in arguing or fighting. . . . Do not be deceived. . . . You can recognize the Spirit of Christ within you when you speak to one another or speak of another person with a warm smile instead of with a frown or scowl.

—Theodore M. Burton
(Ensign, *November 1974, p. 56.*)

Satan's Deadly Aim

During the time between the morning of the First Vision and the night a few years later when the angel Moroni appeared in his room, the Prophet Joseph Smith struggled. He later wrote:

I was left to all kinds of temptations; and, mingling with all kinds of society, I frequently fell into many foolish errors, and displayed the weakness of youth, and the foibles of human nature; which, I am sorry to say, led me into divers temptations, offensive in the sight of God. In making this confession, no one need suppose me guilty of any great or malignant sins. A disposition to commit such was never in my nature. But I was guilty of levity, and sometimes associated with jovial company, etc., not consistent with that character which ought to be maintained by one who was called of God as I had been. (Joseph Smith—History 1:28.)

As with Joseph Smith, there are many good people who have never committed and expect never to commit "great or malignant sins." It is just not part of their disposition or nature. It is these people who are challenged more by "foolish errors" or the "weakness of youth." While none of us can afford to feel secure from sin, it is these people on whom Satan's most likely foothold will be the "foibles of human nature."

Satan's ultimate objective is to corrupt all that is beautiful, good, and peaceful in his efforts to keep us from enjoying the great plan of happiness. He became the master of contention. He knows that with many of God's children contention is the most likely foible, defect, chink, or rust he can put in their "armor." Understanding that this is how Satan works will better enable us to negotiate our way through daily life, speaking with more peace and less contention.

Satan constantly seeks opportunities "to fan into a flame the slightest spark of discontent."[1] As we work within our many relationships we can identify Satan's influence by the pushing and shoving, the competition, the bickering, the friction, and the conflict we see so often. Satan would have us push back, compete, compare, and angrily demand our rights.

Brigham Young addressed this subject on several occasions. He said:

> I will say, there is not a man in this house who has a more indomitable and unyielding temper than myself. But there is not a man in the world who cannot overcome his passion, if he will struggle earnestly to do so. If you find passion coming on you, go off to some place where you cannot be heard; . . . struggle till it leaves you; and pray for strength to overcome.[2]

Dissension is one of Satan's most effective tools, and he does all he can to make us think that anger has some kind of value. If we agree, we have been duped, decoyed, and suckered. Instead we should, in Brigham Young's words, "cast all bitterness out of [our] own hearts—all anger, wrath, strife, covetousness, and lust, and sanctify the Lord God in [our] hearts that [we] may enjoy the Holy Ghost."[3]

Each time we respond with love rather than anger, each time we give a soft reply, it is a victory over Satan.

Brigham Young was frank as to his own battle in this arena: "Though, through the evil that is within me, it is natural for me to contend, and if I am opposed to oppose in return, and if a sharp word is spoken to me to give a sharp word back, I have done so but rarely. It is wrong and we must subdue the inclination."[4] And again, "No man ever did, or ever will rule judiciously on this earth, with honor to himself and glory to his God, unless he first learn to rule and control himself."[5]

President Young poses the question, "Had I not better let it out than to keep it rankling within me?" "No," he responds. "I will keep bad feelings under and actually smother them to death, then they are gone. . . . This is what I call resisting the devil, and he flees from me. I strive to not speak evil, to not feel evil, and if I do, to keep it to myself until it is gone from me, and not let it pass my lips."[6]

Isn't this "smothering" approach an interesting piece of counsel from one of the Lord's prophets, in light of the customary advice of the world that in order to have a more healthy psyche we should vent frustrations? The talk show psychobabble of the day places holding things in as the cause of a national neurosis. There are some, however, who agree with Brother Brigham. In an article in *Psychology Today* Carol Tavris wrote of "Murray Straus, a sociologist in the field of family violence [finding] that 'couples who yell at each other do not thereafter feel less angry but more angry.'" She added, "Talking out an emotion doesn't reduce it, it rehearses it."[7]

In 1859, President Young counseled: "If you are tried and tempted and buffeted by Satan, keep your thoughts to yourselves— keep your mouths closed. . . . If we have light or intelligence . . . we will impart it; but our bad feelings we will keep to ourselves."[8]

Later he further advised: "If you are in the canyon and your cattle are likely to fill you with wrath, fill your mouth with India-rubber and keep it closed that the words cannot get out. Do not say a word to grieve the Spirit of God."9

Satan not only encourages us to vent rather than smother, to lose control and contend, to yell and scream; he also has set an impressive example for us to follow: "And now, when Moses had said these words, Satan cried with a loud voice, and ranted upon the earth, and commanded, saying: I am the Only Begotten, worship me . . . And now Satan began to tremble, and the earth shook. . . . And . . . Satan cried with a loud voice, with weeping, and wailing, and gnashing of teeth. . . ." (Moses 1:19, 21, 22.)

How well Satan modeled the temper tantrum! Have you ever seen someone behave in a somewhat similar fashion? It is not difficult to discern which influence we are following if we act like that, even to a small degree. How we speak to others, especially when under stress, is a measure of which of the two influences we are leaning toward, Satan or Christ.

"Because [Satan] had fallen from heaven, and had become miserable forever, he sought also the misery of all mankind" (2 Nephi 2:18). In other words, misery loves company. Satan is never happier than when he has us fighting, scratching, contending, murmuring, arguing, yelling, and swearing at each other. He delights when our tongues become blender blades. He rejoices as we forsake the higher path and plunge into the swamps of contention.

As we work to master the soft reply, Satan will do all he can to pull us down, deceiving us into thinking that happiness comes from winning at the expense of loving, from personal gain at the expense of service, and from bluntness at the expense of understanding. In this effort he is trying to deceive us into judging "that which is evil to be of God, or that which is good and of God to be of the devil" (Moroni 7:14).

Satan will do anything to have us justify our anger and harsh words. He will never encourage us in gentleness, peaceableness, and sensitivity: "For he persuadeth no man to do good, no, not one;

neither do his angels; neither do they who subject themselves unto him" (Moroni 7:17).

In most situations the tone of our voice can tell us the direction in which we are being led—by Satan toward contention, or by the Savior toward peace. Satan will do all he can to cause us to forget our vision of the eternities and focus only on immediate gratification and conquest.

The Savior never has abandoned and never will abandon us in the "valleys," because he has suffered deeper valleys than any of us could imagine. His atonement will make up for what we lack, as long as we keep trying. But because God has allowed Satan to "tempt and try us," it is well to understand that contention will confront us often. As Elder Russell M. Nelson expressed it: "The work of the adversary may be likened to loading guns in opposition to the work of God. Salvos containing germs of contention are aimed and fired at strategic targets essential to that holy work."[10] And Satan's aim is deadly.

NOTES

1. Brigham Young, in *Journal of Discourses* 12:128. Hereafter cited as *JD*.

2. *JD* 11:290.

3. *JD* 8:33.

4. *JD* 14:149.

5. *JD* 3:256.

6. *JD* 3:195.

7. Carol Tavris, "Anger Defused," *Psychology Today*, November 1982, p. 32.

8. *JD* 7:268.

9. *JD* 12:218.

10. Elder Russell M. Nelson, "The Canker of Contention," *Ensign*, May 1989, p. 69.

CHAPTER 10

*[In] the home in which I lived, . . . there
was a father who, by some quiet magic,
was able to discipline his family without
the use of any instrument of punishment.*

—Gordon B. Hinckley
(Ensign, *November 1978, p. 18.*)

Please Don't Yell

Yelling at someone is like discovering something we can do that doesn't work—so we do it again. "It's time to turn off the TV and come to dinner." No response, so we say it again, only louder. "It's time to turn off the TV and come to dinner." We are just adding volume instead of doing something different. Yelling, like more horses and more men, won't put Humpty together again. Volume and anger, if we yell loud and mean enough, may work. We'll get the bodies to the table, but happy spirits have departed before everyone is seated.

James Allen in *As a Man Thinketh* said, "How many people we know who sour their lives, who ruin all that is sweet and beautiful by explosive [words], who destroy their poise of character, and make bad blood!"[1]

According to the *Ensign's* Handbook for Families, "By raising their voices and acting mad, [verbal bullies] make others give in to them. Unfortunately, as parents use this tactic with their children, the children adopt anger as the way to respond to anything they cannot control."2 That anger goes hand in hand with yelling.

Aside from emergency cries such as "Fire!" or "Stop Thief!" yelling is despicable and offensive. And it is rampant in American families. In many families yelling has become the norm. It happens reflexively. This epidemic is destroying homes and people's lives. You can't read a newspaper or watch a news broadcast without hearing about another "domestic argument" that has ended in domestic violence. One father reported: "I found myself slamming doors and raising my voice . . . and I could see that it would be only a matter of time or degree of anger before I would blow up and do something I really regretted."3

The Lord knows this will happen. He also knows the solution. There has not been a priesthood conference over the past few years in which the Brethren have not reminded priesthood holders how they should behave in their homes. President Gordon B. Hinckley has told priesthood holders: "Perhaps [child abuse] has always been with us but has not received the attention it presently receives. I am glad there is a hue and cry going up against this terrible evil, too much of which is found among our own."4

The Church booklet for ecclesiastical leaders, *Child Abuse*, states: "If any people ought to shun abusive activities and administer comfort and cures for such problems, it should be the Latter-day Saints. Church members should strive to exemplify Christlike attributes in all their relations and avoid cruelty and other inappropriate behavior toward family members and others."5

With few exceptions, abuse begins with words, usually over some form of perceived offense. A bedroom isn't cleaned up, a baby won't stop crying, a spouse forgot to pay a bill. Frustration and anger escalate. Words become more intense. Emotions surge, and violent words are followed by violent actions.

A newspaper headline read: "Father Pleads Guilty in Shaking Death of Toddler."6 He was originally charged with first degree murder but, due to "mitigating" circumstances, was allowed to plead guilty to a reduced charge of manslaughter in the death of his three-year-old daughter in exchange for a reduced sentence. Mitigating circumstances! What were these circumstances that reduced his responsibility in the court's eye? Was the child crying? Had she spilled her milk? Wet the bed? It is difficult to envisage a circumstance that could mitigate such action.

We must remember not to hold our children to a standard beyond their years. If to justify our angry words we were to present such evidence to God as a dish not washed clean, shoes left in front of the TV, or use of all the hot water, would God find this evidence persuasive? Would he agree that yelling was justified?

> What unjust judges fathers are,
> When in regard to us they hold
> That even in our boyish days
> We ought in conduct to be old.[7]

Are there times when children or others need correction? Certainly. Are there times when disciplinary action is necessary? Of course. But is anyone *ever* justified in yelling or inflicting verbal abuse? Never!

NOTES

1. James Allen, *As a Man Thinketh* (Salt Lake City: Bookcraft, n.d.), p. 61.

2. "Handbook for Families: Dealing with Anger and Contention," *Ensign*, September 1988, p. 63.

3. Ibid., p. 62.

4. Gordon B. Hinckley, "To Please Our Heavenly Father," *Ensign*, May 1985, p. 50.

5. In *Child Abuse*, The Church of Jesus Christ of Latter-day Saints, 1985.

6. *Deseret News*, February 24/25, 1992, p. B5.

7. Terence, *The Self-Tormentor*, Act I, Scene 3, translated by F. W. Ricord.

CHAPTER 11

If we all realized that we were the children of one father, we would stop shouting at each other as much as we do.

—*Harold B. Lee, quoting George Bernard Shaw*
(Ensign, *January 1974, p. 6.*)

Content Without Volume

An important revelation on ecclesiastical government that also applies to marriages and families reads:

> No power or influence can or ought to be maintained by virtue of the priesthood, only by persuasion, by long-suffering, by gentleness and meekness, and by love unfeigned;
>
> By kindness, and pure knowledge, which shall greatly enlarge the soul without hypocrisy, and without guile —
>
> Reproving betimes with sharpness, when moved upon by the Holy Ghost; and then showing forth afterwards an increase of love toward him whom thou hast reproved, lest he esteem thee to be his enemy (D&C 121:41–43).

It is sad that many mistakenly use their interpretation of "reproving betimes with sharpness when moved upon by the Holy

Ghost" to excuse or justify harsh words prompted by anger. Elder Neal A. Maxwell explains that *betimes* means *speedily* and *early on*.[1] This suggests that under the influence of the Holy Ghost we could rebuke to nip a certain behavior in the bud, to catch it early, to prevent more of that behavior.

But I see as also important the implication of the dash after the word *guile,* indicating, I suggest, that all the criteria listed in verses 41 and 42 (persuasion, long-suffering, gentleness, meekness, love unfeigned, kindness, the absence of guile, and the absence of hypocrisy) should characterize the attitude of whoever administers the reproof.

The presence of such qualities will "greatly enlarge" not only one's own soul but also the other's soul, especially if pure knowledge is indeed part of the framework. This stated requirement suggests we are likely to have a better effect if we first know what we are talking about.

Too often, volume replaces content or pure knowledge. Reproving betimes with sharpness does not have to involve volume. This scripture is never a license to be angry, raise your voice, or "put down" another.

I have tried to remember this in the form of an algebraic equation: Content $= 1/\text{Volume}$, or the content of anything we say is inversely proportional to the volume. The quieter our reproof, usually, the greater its content. The louder our voice, the less the content. The higher the content and the lower the volume, the more likely it is that relationships will be enhanced, that you will be heard and understood, and that the desired behavior will occur.

I have always tried to think, as I approach a situation of reproof or discipline, "Turn down the volume." Naturally, I haven't always followed my own rule. In fact, I learned this rule the hard way— through negative experiences that I later wanted to undo.

I take comfort, however, from those other occasions when the Spirit was with me and I was able to reply softly. I remember the time that a son, before he had his driver's license, went joyriding in the family car with his friends. Fortunately, he confined his activities to the driveway. I caught him in the act as I drove up to our home, so I had about five seconds to formulate a response. I was really upset as I contemplated the potential risks. I also knew that how I handled this situation would affect our relationship generally and would specifically alter the level of trust we shared about the family cars and teenage driving privileges.

I calmly asked him to get into the car and we cheerfully waved goodbye to his quickly disappearing friends. We drove to a nearby empty parking lot and changed places. I let him practice driving around the empty lot. Afterward I quietly explained my concerns about the driveway incident, but I also offered to take him driving whenever he asked. Legal? I don't know for sure. Safe? Yes. But from then on we didn't have a problem; and when he got his driver's license I felt I could trust him to be a responsible driver, which has saved a lot of worry.

Does turning down the volume work 100 percent of the time? Of course not. But it does dramatically increase our chances of being heard and understood.

Holding the priesthood does not make a man a power broker or allow him to sit on a throne while using his voice like a Black and Decker power tool to rule the family. "Rather, [a priesthood bearer] is a leader by authority of example."[2] "If you love me you will keep my commandments [is far more effective than] if you know what is good for you, you will keep my commandments."[3] "[A father] will listen—even to the smallest child. . . . He will learn to control himself. He will not use a quick temper as an excuse—he will rise above it."[4]

Authoritarianism, like "management by volume," always strains relationships, whether in a family or in any other setting. Children or employees may obey, but it's not any fun and is often done for the wrong reasons.

Yelling, abuse, and uncontrolled anger will never touch the spirit of the listener, especially a child, except in a negative way. In fact, verbal assaults cause that spirit to flee or shut down. How much better to emulate the voice that spoke to the Nephites: "It was not a harsh voice, neither was it a loud voice; nevertheless, and notwithstanding it being a small voice it did pierce them that did hear to the center, insomuch that there was no part of their frame that it did not cause to quake; yea, it did pierce them to the very soul, and did cause their hearts to burn." (3 Nephi 11:3.)

If this is how the Holy Ghost and our Father in Heaven communicate to the very soul of a child, a spouse, or a neighbor, why should we think that turning up the volume will reach into that spirit or soul? It is the difference between using a small key to open the door of the heart as opposed to using a sledgehammer to knock the lock off. I think the Lord expects us to model his style of communication rather than managing by volume.

Here is an excellent example of reproving from a position of pure knowledge rather than by angry volume. Years ago, during a Sunday School discussion of the suffering endured by the members of the Martin Handcart Company in their journey across the plains, an elderly gentleman "arose and said things that no person who heard him will ever forget. . . . He spoke calmly, deliberately, but with great earnestness and sincerity. In substance [he] said":

> I ask you to stop this criticism. . . . Mistake to send the Martin Handcart Company out so late in the season? Yes. But I was in that company. . . . We suffered beyond anything you can imagine and many died of exposure and starvation. . . .
>
> I have pulled my handcart when I was so weak and weary from illness and lack of food that I could hardly put one foot ahead of the other. I have looked ahead and seen a patch of sand or a hill slope and I have said, I can go only that far and there I must give up. . . . I have gone on to that sand and when I reached it, the cart began pushing me. I have looked back many times to see who was pushing my cart, but my eyes saw no one. I knew then that the angels of God were there. . . .

. . . The price we paid to become acquainted with God was a privilege to pay, and I am thankful that I was privileged to come in the Martin Handcart Company.[5]

This reproof was uttered from a standpoint of "pure knowledge." The entire class was instructed, edified, and grateful for what this elderly man taught them.

NOTES

1. See Neal A. Maxwell, *A Wonderful Flood of Light* (Salt Lake City: Bookcraft, 1990), p. 113.

2. James E. Faust, *Ensign*, May 1988, p. 36.

3. See Hugh Nibley, "Leadership Versus Management," *BYU Today*, February 1984, p. 16.

4. H. Burke Peterson, "Priesthood: Authority and Power," *Ensign*, May 1976, p. 33.

5. As quoted in James E. Faust, "The Refiner's Fire," *Ensign*, May 1979, p. 53.

CHAPTER 12

Be strong, my brethren, in the quality of mercy. It is easy to be a bully in one's home, in one's business, in one's speech and acts.

—*Gordon B. Hinckley*
(Ensign, *November 1992, p. 52.*)

Remain Seated . . . Please

One day, Jesus went to the temple, "sat down, and taught them." His lesson was interrupted by scribes and Pharisees who brought into his presence a woman taken in adultery and asked him whether she should be stoned. Instead of answering, Jesus, who was already sitting, "stooped down, and with his finger wrote on the ground, as though he heard them not." Then he looked up and quietly uttered that piercing observation: "He that is without sin among you, let him first cast a stone at her." And then "again he stooped down, and wrote on the ground" until they had all quietly sneaked off. (See John 8:2–11.)

Just as turning down the volume is an effective way to ensure a soft reply, so is sitting down. Jumping up is, verbally speaking, a combat-ready position. I recall how sitting on a log by a campfire, doodling in the dirt or poking at the hot coals, evokes a feeling of meditativeness, reflection, and calm. Deliberately choosing to sit down for a discussion that you think might be a little tense is a good way to automatically defuse the tension.

When a son came home much later than we expected him after an evening with his friends I was beside myself. Every parent knows exactly the combination of worry, anger, and repressed terror that builds as the time ticks away. When he finally came in I surged into his room, relieved yet angry. He was sitting on his chair taking off his shoes. My instinct was to tower over him and launch into the lecture. Instead I knelt down, put my arm on his shoulder, looked him directly in the eye, and asked very quietly, "Do you remember how *you* felt the time we lost your little brother in the Umeda train station in Japan?"

"Yes," he responded, recalling the experience well.

"Well, that's how your mother and I have been feeling for the past two hours worrying about you. Please don't ever do this again. When you can't be home on time, please call or let us know where you are and that you're all right. Okay?" From that night on, he has always done that for us.

I don't know what I would have said had I stood over him. But I do know that I felt different when I was on an eye level with him, almost whispering to him. Try it the next time you're in a situation that you think might get out of hand. Turn down the vocal volume. And turn down the "volume" of your body posture by sitting down.

CHAPTER 13

The words we speak are important.
The Savior taught that men will be
held to account for "every idle word"
in the day of judgment.

—*Dallin H. Oaks*
(Ensign, *May 1986, p. 51.*)

If You Must Speak,
Ask a Question

My wife and I were running a whole series of errands one day; and I, in a hurry to get everything finished, was driving like a Grand Prix wannabe. Margaret's body language was loud and clear. She tightened her seat belt, clung to the hand support over the door, and pressed both feet into the floorboards whenever I put the brakes on. All this told me that she was not very comfortable with the way I was driving.

She didn't say anything, but even so I was tempted to make some smart-aleck remark. I didn't. Instead I tried a useful rule that reduces irritation, lowers the volume, ensures a soft reply, and alleviates contention. It is: If you must speak, ask a question.[1]

"Am I making you nervous?" I asked.

"Yes," she answered.

"Would you like me to slow down?"

"Would you, please?" she asked.

"Okay." I said. I eased off the gas pedal. She relaxed, and we continued on our way.

This minor episode could have ruined the day for both of us if I had decided to communicate with !!!!!s instead of ?????s.

The essence of "If you must speak, ask a question," is embodied in two steps. They may seem awkward at first, but with a little practice they'll merge into one smooth procedure:

Step 1: *Listen with Understanding.*

The biggest block to meaningful communication is not lack of comprehension of the words. It's the mental unwillingness to consider that understanding another's position doesn't necessitate relinquishing your own. To free yourself from this either-or trap, tell yourself: "I will grant this person the right to his/her own position." Then add mentally, "But I also have the right to my own position."

Step 2: *Gather Information with a Question.*

Here are four useful types of questions:

1. Paraphrase or "parrot back" to the other person, in the form of a question, what you understood him/her to say to you. For example: "Son, are you saying you would like to buy a bullet-bike with your savings?"

2. Ask a question, the answer to which contains information that *you* would like to give to the speaker. For example: "How do you think your mom would feel about your having a high-speed bullet-bike?"

3. Ask a question that will create reasonable doubt or introduce an unexplored line of thought into the conversation. For example, "Have you looked into what the insurance surcharge is on bullet-bikes driven by seventeen-year-olds?" Or "Do you have any information about safety records? I talked to a doctor who told me that organ transplant teams call bullet-bikes 'donor bikes.' I wonder why they would say something like that."

4. Ask a question that will defuse potential anger or volatility. For example: "Would you feel all right if I took a day or two to think through this, and then we could both talk about it?"

Remember that in any conversation you cannot truly listen and understand someone else if your mind is busy disagreeing and preparing your rebuttal. Remember that understanding does not mean agreement. You can understand someone else's desire or point of view without agreeing, and you can disagree without being disagreeable. So go ahead, really listen with understanding, and then, when it's your turn to speak, ask a question.

That's it. It's that simple. You'll be amazed at the relaxed atmosphere that can surround conversations, even on difficult topics. You'll be startled at how questions allow a much softer reply because they focus on information rather than on personalities. Questions sidestep the discussion-stopping phenomenon of sitting in judgment. As you use them, both on the job and in your home, communication will improve and relationships will grow. Both youngsters and employees not only will accept correction more easily but also will discover many answers for themselves.

Think of the new avenues of communication and the many voyages of self-discovery triggered by the Savior's gentle questions and comments:

- What manner of men ought ye to be? (3 Nephi 27:27.)
- Where is your treasure? (Matthew 6:21.)
- Who is the greatest among you? (Matthew 23:11.)
- Which of you is without sin? (John 8:7.)
- For if you only love them which love you, what reward have you? (Luke 6:32.)
- How often should I forgive my brother? (Matthew 18:21.)
- What shall it profit a man, if he shall gain the whole world, and lose his own soul? (Mark 8:36.)

In my own attempts to always respond softly to my own friends and family, especially during difficult moments, I have tried to remember the words of this song:

Mine is a home where ev'ry hour
    is blessed by the strength of priesthood pow'r,
With father and mother leading the way,
Teaching me how to trust and obey;
And the things they teach are crystal clear,
*For love is spoken here.*2

NOTES

1. Heard by author in a professional seminar on practice management by Dr. Omer K. Reed, September 1975, in Phoenix, Arizona.

2. "Love Is Spoken Here," *Children's Songbook* (Salt Lake City: The Church of Jesus Christ of Latter-day Saints, 1989), no. 190.

CHAPTER 14

What I am speaking against is any attitude whatever that demeans, that downgrades, that leads to evil speaking of another. In athletic contests there is no occasion for booing and catcalls. Of course mistakes are made by umpires and referees. Of course players do things outside the rules. But the score will not be changed by all the booing in the world.

—*Gordon B. Hinckley*
(Ensign, *November 1981, p. 41.*)

Soft Reply Athletics

Standing on third base is little James. He has failed to technically hit the ball, but the Giants' wily coach, Wayne, employing a classic bit of Little League strategy, had said, "Let's let James get on base," and the other team agreed, because at that point the Giants were losing by a wide margin. That's how James ended up standing on third base for the first time in his life. Next to him, poised ready to coach, is his mother.

Coach Wayne [pitches the ball]. It is a good pitch, bouncing directly off the bat. Bedlam erupts as parents on both teams try to activate their players, but none is shouting with more enthusiasm than [James's mother]. "Run, James!" she yells from maybe a foot away. "Run!"

[Six-year-old] James, startled, looks up, and you can almost see the thought forming in his mind: "I'm supposed to run."

And now he is running, and [Mom] is running next to him, cheering him on, . . . only 15 feet to go, James is about to score his first run ever. Then suddenly, incredibly, . . . there appears . . . the BALL! And . . . an opposing player actually CATCHES it and touches home plate and little James is OUT.

Two things happen. [James's mother] stops [and utters something angrily]. James, oblivious, keeps running. Chugs right on home, touches the plate smiling and wanders off, happy as a clam.[1]

For James, running the bases was his happiness. Whatever those funny guys were doing with the ball was their problem. But for James's mom, the game—and the pleasure—was over. And James's mom has lots of company. I know of one teenager who is glad when his parents don't come to watch him play because of the things they yell during his games.

What is it about sports that makes us so often talk and act as if this moment were the only thing in life that mattered? "Well," one might say, "You remember what Vince Lombardi said! 'Winning isn't everything, it's the only thing.'" The truth, however, is that Coach Lombardi never really said that. As reported in *Sports Illustrated*, an inquisitive sports writer, with a little research, found out what Lombardi really said. It was: "Winning isn't everything, but the effort we make to win, is."

Now, there is a lot of difference between the two expressions. One teaches us we must win at any cost; the other teaches the importance of trying our best. But what does this have to do with the soft reply?

If there was ever an area where we need to control how we talk and where the soft reply would often be a welcome change, it is in sports. The soft reply would be a wonderful substitute for some of the ruthless trash talk we hear or may have used as a spectator, coach, or player—especially when our side is losing.

Normally sane, intelligent, polite, distinguished, reserved, and even deeply spiritual men and women will say and do things during the agony of defeat that are absolutely unthinkable in other contexts. Profanity, obscene gestures, threats, and fists get thrown around like spray on the ocean. Some players deliberately injure their competitors. A soccer player was actually murdered because he accidentally scored a goal for the other team during a World Cup tournament. Spectators are sometimes trampled or wounded during riots surrounding European soccer matches.

Responsible and decent Latter-day Saint priesthood holders undergo a total metamorphosis when they pull on a pair of shorts and hear the referee's whistle blow. Even when they are spectators the distinction between being for a team and being against their opponent suddenly disappears. President Gordon B. Hinckley warned:

> A violent temper is such a terrible, corrosive thing. And the tragedy is that it accomplishes no good; it only feeds evil with resentment and rebellion and pain. To any man or boy within the sound of my voice who has trouble controlling his tongue, may I suggest that you plead with the Lord for the strength to overcome your weakness, that you apologize to those you have offended, and that you marshal within yourselves the power to discipline your tongue. . . .
>
> You may think it is the macho thing to flare up in anger and swear and profane the name of the Lord. It is not the macho thing. It is an indication of weakness. Anger is not an expression of strength. It is an indication of one's inability to control his thoughts, words, his emotions.[2]

President Thomas S. Monson likewise observed:

> In a videotape produced by the Church and entitled *The Church Sports Official,* there is featured this truth from the First Presidency. "Church sports activities have a unique central purpose much higher than the development of physical prowess, or even victory itself. It is to strengthen faith, build integrity, and develop in each participant the attributes of his Maker."

Brethren, it is difficult to achieve this objective if winning overshadows participation. . . . Let's . . . rekindle sportsmanship, to emphasize participation, and to strive for the development of a Christlike character in each individual.[3]

Some may ask, If you are not out there to win, why play? The answer is that there is nothing wrong with playing to win. But nobody wins when winning is the only goal and when harsh words and fits of frustration and outbreaks of anger poison the event.

In one particular ward, a teenage boy with some learning disabilities adored basketball. Between the ages of fourteen and eighteen he played in every basketball game. Whenever he was on the floor, it was a different kind of game. Every player and referee in the stake knew him, loved him, and loved how he loved basketball. Nobody minded that common violations like three-second violations, or traveling, just didn't come up when he played. No matter what was happening in the game, he was always smiling. When he made a basket, the parents and players on both teams cheered. And then, when he was out of the game, it was business as usual.

I have always admired John Wooden, the coach of UCLA's basketball team. His team won ten national championships in twelve years in high-pressure situations, yet he always spoke calmly from the bench, never yelling or even raising his voice at either players or referees.

Jack Hirsch, who played on Wooden's first title team, said: "Wooden isn't the game coach everybody thinks he is. He doesn't have to be. He's so good during the week, he sits back, relaxes and has fun watching the game."[4]

"Soft-reply" athletics has these characteristics: (1) Enthusiasm is always positive. It allows no carping, name-calling, or booing, either as a coach, fan, or participant; (2) It sponsors proper behavior. Check your own behavior by asking yourself, "Would I want my spouse (son, daughter, and so on) to behave like me?"; and (3) You're having fun, and can see the humor in many sports moments.

Even if you're not actually smiling on the inside, you should certainly be smiling on the outside. May I illustrate.

Dick Shultz, who before going into college basketball coaching was a minor league baseball catcher, "once had a manager who was given to eccentric line-up changes."

The manager decided one night to put a rookie third baseman at first base, a position he had never played before. The inevitable happened. A left-handed batter drilled a grounder to the neophyte first baseman, who grabbed the ball and, instead of stepping on the base for the out, reflexively began a throw, quite as if he were playing third. But halfway through the throwing motion he realized where he was and fell into a series of contortions in an effort to keep from throwing the ball away. The runner was so startled by this that he stopped on the baseline. The first baseman finally fired the ball to home plate, where Catcher Shultz made a startled grab.

"I didn't want the ball," Shultz says, "so I threw it back to him."

Although the runner had stopped, the first baseman still did not think to step on first. Instead, he did what a third baseman would do. He cut him off and started a rundown play. The runner, by now as confused as anyone, fell into the act as the first baseman and Shultz began throwing the ball back and forth. Finally the runner made his break back to his last base, which happened to be home. Shultz tagged him, and the umpire bellowed, "You're out!"

Shultz, instead of getting angry, seeing the humorous side of the situation, turned to the umpire and inquired innocently: "What would you have done if he had been safe?"

NOTES

1. Dave Berry, "It's How You Play the Game—Even in the Littlest of Little Leagues," *Deseret News*, March 13, 1988.

2. Gordon B. Hinckley, "Our Solemn Responsibilities," *Ensign*, November 1991, p. 51.

3. Thomas S. Monson, "Goal Beyond Victory," *Ensign*, November 1988, p. 44.

4. Alexander Wolff, "John Wooden," *Sports Illustrated*, September 19, 1994, p. 90.

5. "Scorecard," *Sports Illustrated*, April 5, 1971, pp. 18–19.

CHAPTER 15

*Any man who tries to find humor at the
expense of that which is sacred to another is
deeply flawed in character. Shame on those
who stoop to such actions in the name of
fun and on those who witness and laugh.*

—*Gordon B. Hinckley*
(Ensign, *November 1983, p. 74.*)

Closing the "Hole" to Humor That Bites

At lunch with a group of friends, I heard the following joke:

Once there was a Republican and a Democrat. The Democrat asked: "Why are you a Republican?"

"Because my parents were," answered the Republican.

"That's a silly reason," the Democrat rejoined. "What if your parents were morons?"

"Oh, then I would be a Democrat."

Two members of our group who were quite involved with their respective political parties had been discussing the hot political issue of the day. Being soundly out-debated, one of them, as a final effort to save face, had inserted this story. Everyone laughed at the obvious put-down—even the friend for whom the barb was intended; but I could tell he was hurt by such a cheap shot. It was little comfort that the first debater, realizing that he could not prevail because of the soundness of his facts or the persuasiveness of his reasoning, had shifted the basis of the conversation to a personal attack.

Brigham Young had the right idea when he asked: "Are there any Democrats here? Are there any Republicans here? We do not care who rules; we are satisfied with God, who setteth up one man, and casteth down another."[1] But like my friend, we often insist on casting others down with sarcastic humor. I'm glad that sarcastic barbs based on ethnicity, religion, national origin, and gender are waning in social acceptability—but political humor seems to be increasingly acerbic in recent times.

Some might think that politics is fair game for jokes. While the topic itself offers many opportunities for humor, I don't think personal insults, even in the guise of humor, are anything but discourteous under any circumstances. I remember the hurt feelings my father endured when one of the other brothers in priesthood quorum class jokingly asked how he could be active in the Church, have a son who was a mission president, and still cheer for the University of Utah rather than BYU. I felt hurt on my father's behalf and angry that such "humor" slurred my father's personal righteousness and denigrated something about his family that was special to him.

Humor is a wonderful quality. The joking quip, the quick comeback, or the clever response is an important part of our conversational life, but humorous replies can destroy as well as lift others. The guidelines of using the soft reply welcome all forms of humor as long as it is kind, not edged with contempt or barbed with sarcasm. Insults, even teasing ones, are hard to shrug off; often others who hear a cutting story will pass it on, enjoying the discomfort of another.

In contrast, gentle humor can lift and lighten, focusing on elements of the situation that everyone present can enjoy without anyone feeling hurt. Humor can be the source of many pleasant surprises, adding delight to your day. For example, I remember President Joseph Fielding Smith, standing up to the pulpit in a general conference just after LeGrand Richards had energized the audi-ence with his address. He commented, "We have just listened to a tornado."[2]

I also remember President Howard W. Hunter's saying to the two General Authorities who were helping him sit down after one of his addresses, "You can just drop me anywhere." It focused the humor on himself, not on anyone else, and it was witty because of the double meaning of "drop." Elder Boyd K. Packer lent his arm to an aging LeGrand Richards as they walked to their meeting in the temple together. Elder Richards facetiously asked Elder Packer, "Who is going to help you over when I die of old age?"[3]

Humorous replies can also provide a teaching moment. When President Kimball, then an Apostle, was invited to offer the daily prayer at the United States Senate, there were only six senators on the floor. Someone apologized for the smallness of the group, but President Kimball replied: "That's all right. I was not going to pray to them, anyway."[4]

Humor is also a way of rising above suffering. When President Kimball's son suggested that he take aspirin for his leg pains, Presi-dent Kimball responded that he did not want to take any more pills because he was already "the piller" of the Church.[5]

Such humor is pleasant and uplifting, not spiteful, personal, or mean-spirited. There should be no room in the Latter-day Saint's humor for jokes involving profanity, sexual innuendo, race, ethnic-ity, sacred things, gender, social class, personal appearance, handi-caps, or any other personal aspect. Suzette Haden Elgin, in *You Can't Say That to Me!*, noted that "the highest [TV] ratings and the loudest applause go to the character with the meanest mouth."[6]

When I feel that I might be tempted to use inappropriate humor, I try to remember the experience of the brother of Jared in which he was worried about the design of the barges. What would happen, he asked the Lord, when they went under water? The Lord's response was simple: "And if it so be that the water come in upon thee, behold . . . stop the hole" (see Ether 2:18–20). When a smart comment pops into my mind that has the potential of hurting somebody's feelings, I think: "Close the hole!" Keep that kind of humor from getting out. In other words, don't say it, walk away, bite your tongue, or put your hand over your mouth.

I once made this same point in a stake conference address that was simultaneously being signed for the members of a deaf branch in that stake. I could tell from their faces that they easily related to the topic of the soft reply. When I mentioned the Lord's advice to the brother of Jared, to include these members I added, "And there may be times when it is best for you to put your hands in your pockets." The sister translating my talk demonstrated the point by quickly shoving her hands into her pockets. Instantly, the facial expressions of those wonderful deaf brothers and sisters burst into the most enjoyable laughter I have ever (not heard) seen.

I feel God approves of humor, but it is to lift, to inspire, to love, to comfort, to teach, to thank, and to include. To that end humor can be a blessing to others as well as oneself.

NOTES

1. *JD* 10:329.

2. Lucile Tate, *LeGrand Richards: Beloved Apostle* (Salt Lake City: Bookcraft, 1982), p. 263.

3. Ibid., p. 292.

4. Edward L. Kimball and Andrew E. Kimball Jr., *Spencer W. Kimball* (Salt Lake City: Bookcraft, 1977), p. 419.

5. Ibid., p. 425.

6. Suzette Haden Elgin, *You Can't Say That to Me!* (New York: John Wiley and Sons, 1995), p. 4.

7. Joseph Fielding Smith, *Church History and Modern Revelation* (Salt Lake City: The Church of Jesus Christ of Latter-day Saints, 1947), 1:184–85.

CHAPTER 16

The tongue is the most dangerous, destructive,

and deadly weapon available to man. . . .

We never gain anything or improve our own

character by trying to tear down another.

—*N. Eldon Tanner*

(Ensign, *July 1972, pp. 35, 36.*)

Letting the Lord Steady the Ark

Hugh Nibley has pointed out that "The *Painsville Telegraph* . . . described the family of Smiths as rude, ignorant, simpleminded, gullible, superstitious, and of course sly, scheming, prevaricating, and immoral."[1] There are still those who speak evil of the Brethren.

I think the principle applies to local leaders as well as to General Authorities. Speaking evil of our leaders violates the spirit of the soft reply. Furthermore, it is futile because its only real effect is to cause the listener to perceive the speaker differently. It very seldom changes anyone's mind about the person being spoken evil of. Evil speaking can also become very contentious. The fact that one may be talking "about" someone rather than directly "to" someone does not change the meanness or adversarial spirit of one's words.

Brother Nibley tells us that Joseph Smith could take in his stride negative things said to or about him because he "had been tutored from above, [and] reached a conclusion: 'The opinions of men, so far as I am concerned, are to me as the crackling of the thorns under the pot, or the whistling of the wind.' "[2] The General Authorities may well have a similar outlook as they administer the affairs of the Church in a modern fish-bowl world.

Individuals may disagree with the Church's stand on lotteries, abortion, homosexuality, parimutuel betting, moral standards, dress codes, pornography, shopping on Sunday, R-rated movies, a smoke-free environment, working mothers, a new missionary policy, and liquor laws. On the local level individuals may also disagree with a new ward or stake boundary, a new athletic policy, or how a particular Sunday School class is run. It is very easy in such cases for individuals to temporarily set aside more foundational knowledge and testimony, depart from a discussion of the issue itself, and take out their frustrations and disappointments on the officers who they think initiated the policy with which they disagree. Brethren-bashing and Brethren-blaming may erupt when the policy challenges a personal gospel hobby, interrupts a lifestyle, or has some kind of personal economic consequence. Often the motive behind such evil-speaking is as transparent as shrink wrap and just as difficult to remove.

Brother Nibley reminds us that "what the Brethren say is the word and the will of the Lord" (cf. D&C 84), but only, "as President [J. Reuben] Clark pointed out no less than twenty-seven times in a speech on the subject, when they are so moved upon by the Holy Ghost." The logical question then arises, "How can we know that?"[3]

The answer: "By following the oft-repeated principle that everyone must so live that the Holy Ghost will reveal to him whether the others are speaking by the Spirit or not." Brother Nibley then quotes Brigham Young: "I have a request to make of each and every Latter-day Saint, or those who profess to be, to so live that the Spirit of the Lord will whisper to them and teach them the truth."[4]

A glorious aspect of this gospel is that we have never been and never will be asked to just take someone's word for it, because if we are living worthily, we have been promised individual revelation. The Lord—if we "ask with a sincere heart, with real intent" (Moroni 10:4)—will ratify the doctrine, the policy, or the administrative issue about which we are concerned.

Rather than speaking evil of any leader, cutting ourselves off from the Spirit, or creating disharmony in our relationships with others, we should seek our own revelation or witness concerning the matter before we speak, and develop the attitude that the Prophet Joseph commended to us when he said: "The Lord steadies the ark. If it does . . . appear to need steadying . . . or something to all appearance threatens its overthrow, be careful how you stretch forth your hands to steady it." We are better off, as Joseph Smith stated, to "be faithful and silent" at such times.5

Brother Nibley adds his commentary: "So what do you do if you see folly and error all around you? You continue to think for yourself. That's the first rule, which means to think *to* yourself." He adds: "The Brethren have their work cut out for them, and strenuous work it is. It calls for studying the gospel, and seeing that the greatest possible number of people in all parts of the world get to hear the first principles. This requires constant repetition of first principles to fresh audiences wherever General Authorities go."6

My callings as a stake president, as a mission president, and as a Regional Representative have brought me into contact with many of the Brethren at conferences, on planes and trains, and in automobiles. I agree with Brother Nibley that theirs is not an easy task. Yet in spite of human weakness and error—both of which will always exist—I also agree with Brother Nibley that

overriding all else is that grand feeling of love which makes life a joy, and everything I read about Joseph Smith reflects that promise. "I see no faults in the church," he said, "Let me be resurrected with the Saints, whether to heaven or hell." . . . A particular fault is neither here or there. . . . "Friendship is the grand fundamental principle of Mormonism, to revolution[ize and] civilize the world, [to] pour forth love. . . . I do not dwell upon your faults. You shall not [dwell] upon mine."7

I have felt that same love and friendship myself. I feel that I could never say anything unkind or return anything but a soft reply where the Brethren are concerned. If I see something a little differently, I must continue to help build the kingdom in a positive, constructive way, with the faith that the Lord will "steady the ark" if it needs steadying.

Hugh Nibley tells of a delightful experience:

> I spent a week with Apostle Spencer W. Kimball visiting his home state in Arizona. We were gone ten days. We went by train in those early days. We came back to the old Los Angeles station, and in that part of Los Angeles, there were a lot of bookstores, which I knew very well. I bought a whole set, a very rare collection, of Alfonsus De Lingorio, the seventeenth-century Redemptorist writer on probabilism, a very valuable set of ten volumes. I barely made it back to the train by running across a lot. I jumped on the train, plunked down beside Brother Kimball, who was already on the train, and staggered into the drawing room, my arms full of the complete set, which I greatly valued.
>
> As we sat talking about the books, Brother Kimball casually took an immaculate linen handkerchief from the breast pocket of his jacket, and, stooping over, vigorously dusted off my shoes and trousers. It was the most natural thing in the world, and we both took it completely for granted. . . . It was no great thing—*pas d'histoire.* Neither of us said a thing about it, but ever since, that has conditioned my attitude toward the Brethren. I truly believe that they are chosen servants of God.8

NOTES

1. Hugh Nibley, "Criticizing the Brethren," Nibley Archive (Provo, Utah: F.A.R.M.S., 1989), p. 1.

2. Ibid., p. 2.

3. Ibid., p. 12.

4. Ibid., p. 12, quoting *JD* 17:51.

5. As quoted in ibid., p. 17.

6. Ibid., pp. 17, 21.

7. Ibid., p. 22.

8. Hugh Nibley, *Brother Brigham Challenges the Saints* (Salt Lake City: Deseret Book Company, 1994), p. 444.

CHAPTER 17

Contention . . . drives the Spirit of the Lord away. . . .

Contention ranges from a hostile spoken word to

worldwide conflicts.

—*Ezra Taft Benson*
(Ensign, *May 1989, p. 6.*)

Order Out of Chaos

As a young husband, father, and involved career-beginner, I was what you could call a "day-planner-templegoer." Going to the temple appeared on my list at regular intervals and was checked off with dutiful satisfaction. I was usually more concerned with where Margaret and I would eat afterwards than with the spiritual dining within the temple. I listened with a degree of envy as people bore their testimonies about how they loved going to the temple and looked forward to it. But early on, for me, real life with all its frustrations was lived outside the temple, and there wasn't much carryover.

One day, however, after a particularly hectic week, as I entered the temple a little sign in the foyer happened to catch my attention. It reminded people to communicate quietly in order to maintain the peaceful spirit that should exist in the temple. That seemed like an easy enough request while in the temple, but I wondered momentarily why it was so difficult outside the temple for me to always communicate in that same way.

With that reminder on my mind, that evening I experienced an unexpected series of intuitive leaps, both by learning and by remembering, that linked the house of the Lord, with its spirit and endowment, to my life outside the temple and the spirit I wanted to have in my home, with my family, at work, or wherever. The temple experience became personally relevant to a specific challenge in my life. Ever since, I have sought the influence of the temple in my life with the anticipation of which I had heard others speak.

That day the temple experience and the soft reply became connected. It's like this: I remembered how the scientific concept of entropy describes the tendency of all matter (our temperaments as well) to become increasingly disorganized at times. Mental and spiritual entropy is evidenced by the frustration, anger, impatience, and discontent we begin to exhibit and act out because of problems and challenges that life "dishes" out each day. But in the temple we learn of a countering force that restores and maintains order in the universe. Hugh Nibley put it this way:

> The normal state of matter is chaos, always and forever. [God organized matter into our world], bringing order from chaos. It would be a fairy story if we didn't have a world to prove it. . . . Once organized, the protons should long ago have broken down. But, here we are.
>
> The temple represents that organizing principle in the universe that brings all things together. Why did the Egyptians build temples? The Egyptians felt themselves surrounded by an omni-present and ever-threatening chaos. They were intensely conscious of the second law of breaking down. . . .
>
> The temple represents the principle of order in the universe.[1]

The temple experience offers a time for mental and spiritual restoration. It offers a reordering, a reorganization, and a relearning of eternal principles, perspectives, and priorities to help us deal with a world outside the temple, which is governed by spiritual and social entropy, breakdown, anger, and contention. Exposed routinely to the frothy flotsam of news about war, money, violence, sex, hate, crime, competition, and anger, we often find it difficult not to become worn down, impatient, less loving—in short, part of the problem. The temple experience gives personal meaning to the Lord's counsel to the Prophet Joseph Smith in prison, wherein He said: "Peace be unto thy soul; thine adversity and thine afflictions shall be but a small moment" (D&C 121:7).

What greater source of strength, reordering, reprieve, and refocusing on what is really important could there be than the temple? The temple will bring order out of chaos and softness out of a harsh world. The dedicatory prayer of the Kirtland Temple asks that "all people who shall enter upon the threshold of the Lord's house may feel thy power and feel constrained" (D&C 109:13).

Similarly we may pray to have the constraint that will enable us to maintain poise and patience with each other, our family, a neighbor, a boss, an employee, another driver, or even a referee—if we will seek the peace and perspective of the temple. Chaos and frustration in our life can give way to order, and the soft reply can become a stable part of our communication not only while inside but while outside the temple as well.

NOTES

1. Hugh Nibley, "The Meaning of the Temple" (Provo, Utah: F.A.R.M.S., 1975), pp. 9, 11.

Husbands and wives need . . . to keep

always open between them a gentle and

frank and kindly communication.

—*Richard L. Evans*

(Improvement Era, *December 1963, p. 1075.*)

CHAPTER 18

With Tongues of Angels

Scriptural expressions like "O that I were an angel" (Alma 29:1) and "after ye had received the Holy Ghost ye could speak with the tongue of angels" (2 Nephi 32:2) have often made me wonder what it would actually be like to be able to speak in the manner of an angel. I appreciate Oliver Cowdery's description of what it was like for him to listen to an angel, since it gives me a sense of the ultimate power of the soft reply:

Our eyes beheld, our ears heard. . . . Then his voice, though mild, pierced to the center, and his words "I am thy fellow-servant," dispelled every fear. We listened, we gazed, we admired! 'Twas the voice of an angel from glory. . . .

I shall not attempt to paint to you the feelings of this heart, nor the majestic beauty and glory which surrounded us on this occasion; but you will believe me when I say, that earth, nor men, with the eloquence of time, cannot begin to clothe language in as interesting and sublime a manner as this holy personage. No; nor has this earth power to give the joy, to bestow the peace, or comprehend the wisdom which was contained in each sentence as they were delivered by the power of the Holy Spirit! (Joseph Smith—History 1:71, footnote.)

What a miracle it would be if we were able to cause others to feel, even in a small way, the way this angel caused Oliver to feel! Yet some on earth have managed to speak as angels do.

The soft reply represents an effort to develop more angelic dialogue. Angelic discourse is filled with the pure love of Christ, which we have been instructed to seek "with all the energy of heart" (Moroni 7:48). Angelic discourse can never be a "bitter fountain" (see Moroni 7:11). As we achieve this level of discourse we will not speak harsh words, because they will not be part of our nature. The internal will become eternal. At moments of special need, we will speak with the "tongues of angels."

CHAPTER 19

In his The Prince of Peace, *William Jennings Bryan wrote: "The most difficult of all the virtues to cultivate is the forgiving spirit. Revenge seems to be natural with man; it is human to want to get even with an enemy. It has even been popular to boast of vindictiveness; it was once inscribed on a man's monument that he had repaid both friends and enemies more than he had received. This was not the spirit of Christ."*

—*Spencer W. Kimball*
(Ensign, *November 1977, p. 48.*)

The Spoken Light of a Soft Reply

The best example of one who exemplified the soft reply is the Savior. Rich with truth and content, always thought provoking, His words modeled a quality of conversation we should all try to achieve. His was a quality of conversation that projected light into the lives of others. "For the word of the Lord is truth, and whatsoever is truth is light, and whatsoever is light is Spirit, even the Spirit of Jesus Christ" (D&C 84:45).

Robert Fulghum tells of his experience with a lecturer, Alexander Papaderos, who as a boy had made from broken pieces a mirror that would reflect sunlight into dark places that never directly received sunshine. As he matured, this childhood discovery had become a metaphor for what he could do with life.[1]

This has much relevance for Latter-day Saints. Like the Savior, we can use gentle words and pose thoughtful questions. Our own soft replies will reflect His light into the hearts of others, because as we show our concern and sensitivity we can invite a spirit of Christlike love and understanding into any conversation. We can never go wrong when following Jesus' example. The soft reply will always have a better chance of lifting others as we model His "love," His "truth," His "light" and His "spirit," in our conversations. We become a Christlike mirror or a beacon to other people.

I hope I can live up to the respect President Hinckley expressed "for fathers and mothers who are nurturing their children in light and truth . . . who spare the rod and govern with love."[2]

Each of us too can be a mirror, reflecting into the lives of our family and others the Savior's light. Soft replies, quiet answers, and peaceful responses become forms of spoken light and Christlike love.

NOTES

1. See Robert Fulghum, *It Was on Fire When I Lay Down on It* (New York: Villard Books, 1989), pp. 175–77.

2. Gordon B. Hinckley, "This Is the Work of the Master," *Ensign,* May 1995, p. 70.

CHAPTER 20

*How are we supposed to act when we are offended, mis-
understood, unfairly or unkindly treated, or sinned
against? What are we supposed to do if we are hurt by
those we love, or passed over for promotion, or are falsely
accused, or have our motives unfairly assailed? Do we
fight back? Do we send in an ever-larger battalion? Do
we revert to an eye for an eye and a tooth for a tooth, or,
as Tevye says in* Fiddler on the Roof, *do we come to
the realization that this finally leaves us blind and toothless?*

—*Howard W. Hunter*
(Ensign, *November 1992, p. 18.*)

The Law of Least Effort

There is an age-old philosophy known as the principle of economy of effort, or do less and accomplish more. My mission of discovery about the soft reply was helped enormously when I understood how this principle, the law of least effort, applied to the soft reply.

Let me explain. Anything we do in our life, if motivated by love, has no wasted energy. When our actions are motivated by love our energy actually multiplies and is synergistic. On the contrary, whenever we seek power and control over other people we waste energy.

When you choose a soft answer, which I feel is a loving act, you use the law of least effort because very little or no time and energy has to be wasted afterwards in "damage control" such as is necessary to heal or mend a strained relationship. A soft reply means that we understand that our attempt at an un-soft "cure" is worse than the "disease."

When you use a harsh or mean-spirited reply, you frequently spend much energy, time, worry, anguish, guilt, and effort afterwards in making right something that didn't have to be in the first place.

With a Christlike reply you reach out, help, and nurture. It is really the easiest path, and overall it requires the least effort. On the other hand, giving attention and focus to your ego, posturing, image enhancement, defending your point of view, or seeking power, control, or approval from others—this spends energy in a wasteful way. Deepak Chopra writes: "In *The Art of Dreaming* Don Juan tells Carlos Castaneda, '. . . most of our energy goes into upholding our importance. . . . If we were capable of losing some of that importance, . . . we would free our energy from trying to maintain the illusory idea of our grandeur.' "[1]

If you can rise above the need to always defend your point of view, there is no frustration. It is frustration that often leads to anger. Anger makes a soft reply very difficult. There are times when you must stand up for what you believe, but even at those times there is a loving way to do it.

Deepak Chopra summarized the law of least effort with these words: "When you feel frustrated or upset by a person or a situation, remember that you are not reacting to the person or the situation, but to your feelings about the person or the situation. These are *your* feelings, and your feelings are not someone else's fault. When you recognize and understand this completely, you are ready to take responsibility for how you feel and to change it. . . . Responsibility . . . means the *ability* to have a creative *response* to the situation."[2]

In many situations a soft reply will require you to relinquish your need to defend, or convince others of, your point of view. It is so easy to lash back, but when the Savior "answered them not," and did not call down the angels of heaven to destroy His abusers, He exemplified the law of least effort. He had the power to overcome them all, but His unwavering commitment to the Atonement and the love it would demonstrate to all mankind was superior to any fleeting gratification, such as we ourselves might have enjoyed from taking a moment to "clean house" on our accusers to preserve our ego. In the long term it is always easier to love. It always takes more effort to clean up after a spiteful relapse.

The law of least effort requires that we keep our eye on the big picture. If we do, we will become more immune to criticism, unafraid of any challenge, able to harness the power of Christlike love, and master of the soft reply.

NOTES

1. Deepak Chopra, *The Seven Spiritual Laws of Success* (San Rafael, CA: Amber Allen Publishing, 1994), p. 56.

2. Ibid., pp. 58–59.

CHAPTER 21

Peace was on the lips and in the heart of the Savior no matter how fiercely the tempest was raging.

—*Howard W. Hunter*
(Ensign, November 1984, p. 35.)

Peace, Be Still

We can all progress in making the soft reply a part of our nature most of the time. Unlike the Savior—who exemplified the ability to submit the tendencies of the flesh to the Spirit and *never* take offense, *never* feel insulted, and *never* want to fight back—we may not reach that degree of perfection in this life. But without the soft reply it is a simple fact that we will never become as Christlike as we someday hope to become. Indeed, He suffered "afflictions and temptations of every kind" (Alma 7:11) and "pain of body, hunger, thirst, and fatigue, even more than man can suffer, except it be unto death" (Mosiah 3:7).

In a devotional address at Brigham Young University, Terry Warner taught that no one had more justification to respond to others in a less than loving manner than the Savior. No one had more reason to rebuke, scold, or react in such "oh-so-human" ways than did the Savior, but he did not do these things. He endured, often without saying anything and without taking offense or retaliating. Suffering more humiliation than any group of minorities, including African Americans, Native Americans, the victims of the Holocaust, and the early Saints in Missouri, the Savior felt no vindictiveness; his love for those whose sins he would bear and atone for never diminished. Unlike the Savior, when we respond to others for any reason in a less than kind manner, others feel used and slighted by this form of subtle violence. When we are tempted to speak harshly in volume or content in any circumstance, like the Savior we must strive to resist.

Quoting Brother Warner directly:

> [The Savior] defeated all the pressures that push humanity toward enmity and discord. He absorbed the terrible poison of vengeance into himself and metabolized it by his love. . . .
>
> This long-suffering love changes everything. . . . For if we heed its invitation, we are stopped short in our arrogance. . . . We are humbled in our pride or anger or selfishness.
>
> How then shall we come unto Christ . . . ? By sacrificing all taking of offense. By giving up criticism, impatience, and contempt, for they accuse the sisters and brothers for whom Christ died.[1]

When I am angry and tempted to speak in a manner less than Christlike, at that moment, a moment in my life when I might actually "come unto Christ," three important words often make the difference between a soft reply and a harsh one. They are found in the story of the disciples aboard the ship in the Sea of Galilee with the Savior.

> And there arose a great storm of wind, and the waves beat into the ship, so that it was now full.
>
> And he was in the hinder part of the ship, asleep on a pillow: and they awake him, and say unto him, Master, carest thou not that we perish?

And he arose, and rebuked the wind, and said unto the sea, Peace, be still. And the wind ceased, and there was a great calm. (Mark 4:37–39.)

Like the disciples, on that occasion, we sometimes feel the winds and the waves swell within us to the point at which we are full of anger or frustration or impatience. But we need to conquer these feelings. And if not conquer them, never act on them. To do so is a terrible thing.

In the Sunday morning session of general conference October 1996 President Hinckley admonished brethren who "put on a fine face before the world during the day and come home in the evening, set aside their self-discipline, and on the slightest provocation fly into outbursts of anger." Using the word *rebuke*, he chastised and called to repentance those who become angry over things of "small consequence," causing others to fear them, and said "no man who engages in such evil and unbecoming behavior is worthy of the priesthood of God." He continued: "What a terrible price you are paying for your anger. Ask the Lord to forgive you, ask your wife to forgive you. Apologize to your children."[2]

There is a place in the hinder part of our minds and hearts into which we often push love, reason, and common sense when we are angry. Yet when we feel the turmoil and know that our feelings are about to surge forth as uncontrolled harshness, we have the ability to awake the Master within us and quiet the storms of the soul.

James Allen eloquently wrote: "Tempest-tossed souls, wherever ye may be, under whatsoever conditions ye may live. . . . keep your hand firmly upon the helm of thought. In the bark of your soul reclines the commanding Master; He does but sleep; wake Him. . . . Say unto your heart, 'Peace, be still.'"[3]

When the temptation to speak harshly flickers, the thought "Peace, be still," repeated to myself as quietly and as rapidly as a prayer, reaches into my mind and awakens a greater power. My expressions, instead of being tumultuous, become kind. This will happen more and more as we seek to become the kind of person the disciples described when they asked, "What manner of man is this, that even the wind and the sea obey him?" (Mark 4:41). That's the kind of person we should all hope to become.

During the sudden storms of our lives, the words "Peace, be still" might awake the mastering spirit of Christlike love, protecting those who love and trust us and subduing the winds and the waves of our soul. Thus we can welcome in our lives the miracle of the soft reply.

NOTES

1. See C. Terry Warner, "Honest, Simple, Solid, True," *Brigham Young Magazine*, June 1996, pp. 35–37.

2. Gordon B. Hinckley, "Women of the Church," *Ensign*, November 1996, p. 68.

3. James Allen, *As a Man Thinketh* (Salt Lake City: Bookcraft, n.d.) p. 62.

Index

About the Author

For twenty-seven years Barlow L. Packer has been practicing dentistry in the Salt Lake area. He is the coauthor, with Boyd C. Matheson, of *Put Yourself on Paper: The Warmth, Power, and Influence of Handwritten Expression.* He has served as a stake president and Regional Representative and has also been president of the Japan Kobe Mission.

Brother Packer is married to Margaret Gardiner Packer, and they are the parents of five children. The family resides in Salt Lake City.